The Ultimate Crock Pot Cookbook

2000 Days of Flavorful Recipes – Master Slow Cooking for Beginners with Easy, Healthy, and Delicious Creations – Your Guide to Unleashing Crock Pot Magic!

Caraphina Hartwell

Table of Contents

INTRODUCTION

What Is Crock-Pot?

The Crock-Pot, a trademarked brand of slow cooker, has become synonymous with convenient and versatile cooking. Essentially, a Crock-Pot is an electrical cooking appliance designed to simmer food at a low temperature for an extended period, making it an excellent tool for slow cooking and tenderizing meats, as well as infusing flavors into various dishes.

The Crock-Pot consists of three main components: a base unit, a removable cooking pot, and a lid. The base unit houses the heating element, controls, and sometimes a digital timer. The removable cooking pot is typically made of stoneware or ceramic, materials that can withstand prolonged heat exposure. The lid is an essential part of the Crock-Pot, creating a sealed environment that traps heat and moisture, contributing to the slow-cooking process.

The hallmark of a Crock-Pot is its ability to cook food over an extended period, usually ranging from a few hours to even an entire day. The low and slow cooking method allows for the gradual breakdown of tough connective tissues in meats, resulting in tender and flavorful dishes. This approach is particularly well-suited for cuts of meat that benefit from slow cooking, such as roasts, stews, and braises.

Crock-Pots are incredibly user-friendly. They usually have simple controls, often featuring settings like High, Low, and Warm. The programmable nature of modern Crock-Pots allows users to set specific cooking times and temperatures, providing flexibility for various recipes. The digital timer on models like the Crock Pot Programmable Cook & Carry Slow Cooker allows for precise customization, ensuring that your meals are cooked to perfection.

The portability of Crock-Pots is another defining feature. Models like the Crock Pot Programmable Cook & Carry Slow Cooker are designed for on-the-go use. The secure locking lid and rubber gasket create an airtight seal, preventing spills during transportation. This makes Crock-Pots ideal for potlucks, family gatherings, tailgating events, and parties. The ability to prepare meals at home and transport them without a hassle adds a layer of convenience to busy lifestyles.

Crock-Pots have a wide range of applications in the kitchen. They excel not only at preparing hearty stews and roasts but also at making soups, chili, casseroles, and even desserts. The slow and gentle cooking process enhances the blending of flavors, allowing ingredients to meld together and create rich, savory dishes. The

versatility of Crock-Pots makes them suitable for various culinary preferences and dietary restrictions.

In summary, a Crock-Pot is a slow cooker designed for easy, convenient, and flavorful cooking. Its simple yet effective design, with a base unit, removable cooking pot, and lid, allows for the slow cooking of a variety of dishes. The programmable features, such as digital timers and temperature settings, enhance the user experience, while the portability makes it a practical choice for those who want to prepare meals at home and enjoy them on the go. Whether you're a busy professional, a home cook with a hectic schedule, or someone who appreciates the art of slow cooking, a Crock-Pot is a valuable kitchen companion.

The Major Benefits of the Crock Pot

The Crock Pot, or slow cooker, has become a staple in many kitchens, offering a myriad of benefits that cater to the needs and preferences of modern-day cooks. From convenience to versatility, the major advantages of using a Crock Pot contribute to its widespread popularity.

- Time Efficiency:

  One of the primary benefits of a Crock Pot is its ability to save time for busy individuals or families. The slow cooking process allows you to prepare ingredients in the morning, set them in the Crock Pot, and return later in the day to a fully cooked, delicious meal. This is particularly advantageous for those with demanding schedules who still want to enjoy homemade, nutritious meals without spending hours in the kitchen.

- Tenderizing Tough Cuts of Meat:

  The slow and low-temperature cooking method of a Crock Pot is perfect for tenderizing tough cuts of meat. Cheaper and more robust cuts, which may be less desirable when cooked quickly, transform into succulent, flavorful dishes after hours of slow cooking. This is due to the gradual breakdown of collagen and connective tissues, resulting in meats that are fork-tender and infused with rich flavors.

- Flavorful and Nutrient-Rich Meals:

  Crock Pots excel at intensifying flavors and melding ingredients together. The extended cooking time allows herbs, spices, and seasonings to fully permeate the dish, creating a depth of flavor that is often hard to achieve with faster cooking methods. Additionally, the sealed environment of the Crock Pot helps retain nutrients in the food, ensuring that your meals are not only delicious but also nutritious.

- Set It and Forget It Convenience:

The "set it and forget it" nature of a Crock Pot is a major convenience factor. Once you've loaded the ingredients and set the desired temperature and cooking time, you can go about your day without worrying about monitoring the cooking process. This hands-off approach is especially valuable for individuals who are not able to spend a lot of time in the kitchen or prefer a hassle-free cooking experience.

- Versatility in Cooking:

  Crock Pots are incredibly versatile and can be used to prepare a wide variety of dishes. From hearty stews and soups to chili, casseroles, and even desserts, the slow cooker can handle an array of recipes. This versatility makes it a valuable tool for home cooks looking to diversify their menu without investing in multiple kitchen appliances.

- Economical Cooking:

  Using a Crock Pot can be a budget-friendly way to prepare meals. The slow cooking process allows you to make the most of less expensive cuts of meat, which tend to be more flavorful but require longer cooking times to become tender. Additionally, Crock Pots are energy-efficient, often using less electricity compared to traditional ovens or stovetop cooking methods.

- Portability for On-the-Go Meals:

  The portability feature, as exemplified by the Crock Pot

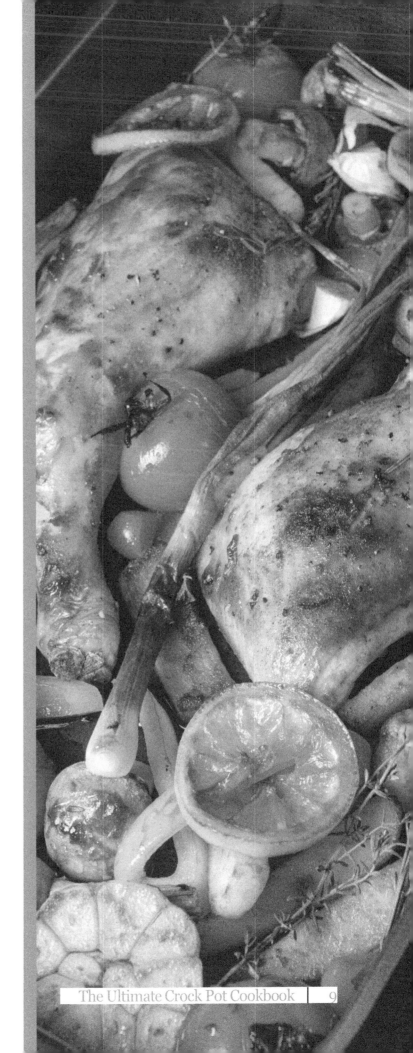

Programmable Cook & Carry Slow Cooker, adds another layer of convenience. The secure locking lid and rubber gasket create an airtight seal, preventing spills during transportation. This makes Crock Pots ideal for taking dishes to potlucks, family gatherings, tailgating events, and parties, allowing you to share homemade meals without the worry of mess or spills.

- Easy Cleanup:

Many Crock Pot models, including the one mentioned, come with dishwasher-safe components. The removable cooking pot and lid can be easily cleaned in the dishwasher, streamlining the cleanup process and making the Crock Pot a user-friendly appliance.

- Healthier Cooking with Less Oil:

The slow cooking process in a Crock Pot often eliminates the need for excessive amounts of oil or fats. Ingredients release their natural juices during the extended cooking time, creating moist and flavorful dishes without the need for added fats. This makes Crock Pot cooking a healthier option for those who are conscious of their fat intake.

- Ideal for Batch Cooking and Meal Prep:

Crock Pots are excellent tools for batch cooking and meal prep. With their generous capacity, you can prepare large quantities of food at once, allowing for multiple servings or the creation of freezer-friendly meals. This is particularly beneficial for individuals or families who want to plan and organize their meals in advance.

In conclusion, the major benefits of a Crock Pot make it a valuable addition to any kitchen. From time efficiency and tenderizing tough cuts of meat to flavorful and nutrient-rich meals, the Crock Pot caters to a variety of cooking needs. Its versatility, set-it-and-forget-it convenience, and portability contribute to its popularity among home cooks seeking efficient and delicious ways to prepare a wide range of dishes. Whether you're a busy professional, a home chef with a hectic schedule, or someone looking for an easy and economical cooking solution, the Crock Pot offers a host of advantages that enhance the overall cooking experience.

How to Choose a Suitable Time?

The Crock Pot Programmable Cook & Carry Slow Cooker with Digital Timer

offers a wide range of cooking times, from as short as 30 minutes to as long as 20 hours. Choosing the right cooking time is crucial for ensuring that your food is perfectly cooked, flavorful, and safe to eat. Here are some guidelines to help you select a suitable time for your slow cooking:

- Type of Ingredients:

  Consider the type of ingredients you're using. Tougher meats and root vegetables generally require longer cooking times to become tender and fully cooked. On the other hand, more delicate ingredients like fish or certain vegetables might need shorter cooking durations to avoid overcooking and maintain their texture.

- Recipe Recommendations:

  Refer to your recipe book for specific guidelines on cooking times. The Crock Pot's programmable feature allows you to follow recipes precisely. If you're new to slow cooking, it's advisable to start with tried-and-true recipes provided in the cookbook to get a sense of the appropriate cooking times for various dishes.

- Desired Texture and Flavor:

  Consider the texture and flavor you want to achieve. Longer cooking times often result in more tender meats and enhanced flavor as the ingredients have more time to meld together. However, if you prefer a fresher taste and firmer texture, opt for shorter cooking times.

- Meal Planning:

  Plan your meals ahead of time to determine the best cooking duration. If you're preparing a dish for a specific mealtime, calculate the hours leading up to that moment to ensure your meal is ready when you need it. The programmable feature allows you to set the cooker to start at a later time, providing convenience for busy schedules.

- Crock Pot Size and Capacity:

  The size and capacity of your Crock Pot can influence cooking times. Larger quantities of food may require additional time to cook thoroughly. Conversely, smaller portions may cook faster. Be mindful of the size of your slow cooker and adjust cooking times accordingly.

- Experiment and Adjust:

  Slow cooking is as much an art as it is a science. Don't be afraid to experiment with cooking times. If you find that a recipe is consistently undercooked or overcooked, adjust the time accordingly in subsequent attempts. Keep notes on your cooking times and outcomes to refine your skills.

- Temperature Settings:

  Take advantage of the Crock Pot's temperature settings—High, Low, and Warm. High is for faster cooking, while Low is for a longer, slower cook. The Warm setting is ideal for keeping your food at a safe and enjoyable temperature after the initial cooking process.

In conclusion, choosing a suitable time for your Crock Pot cooking involves a combination of understanding your ingredients, following recipe

recommendations, considering desired outcomes, planning, and a bit of experimentation. The programmable feature of your slow cooker adds a layer of convenience, allowing you to customize cooking times to suit your schedule and preferences. As you become more familiar with your Crock Pot, you'll develop a sense of the optimal cooking times for various dishes.

Crucial Tips for Successful Crock-Pot Cooking

Slow cooking with the Crock Pot Programmable Cook & Carry Slow Cooker can result in flavorful and tender dishes with minimal effort. To ensure success in your slow-cooking endeavors, consider the following crucial tips:

- Prep Ingredients in Advance:

  Prepare and chop your ingredients the night before or in the morning to save time when it's cooking time. This not only streamlines the process but also allows flavors to meld together more effectively during the slow-cooking process.

- Searing Meats for Flavor:

  While not mandatory, searing meats before placing them in the slow cooker can enhance the flavor of your dish. Searing caramelizes the surface of the meat, adding depth and complexity to the final flavor. It's an extra step that can make a significant difference.

- Layer Ingredients Wisely:

  Proper layering is essential for even cooking. Place root vegetables at the bottom, followed by meats, and top it off with more delicate ingredients. This arrangement ensures that denser items receive more heat and cook thoroughly.

- Don't Overfill the Crock Pot:

Avoid overfilling the slow cooker. To ensure even cooking and to prevent spills, fill the Crock Pot between one-half and two-thirds full. This allows enough space for the ingredients to cook properly and minimizes the risk of overflowing.

- Mind the Liquid Levels:

  Liquids don't evaporate as much in slow cookers as they do in traditional cooking methods. Adjust the amount of liquid in your recipes accordingly. If in doubt, start with less liquid and add more later if needed. Too much liquid can result in a watery dish.

- Follow Layering Instructions:

  Some recipes may provide specific instructions on layering ingredients. Follow these instructions closely for the best results. For example, placing rice or pasta at the top might lead to overcooking, so it's essential to follow the recipe's layering guidance.

- Avoid Constant Opening of the Lid:

  Every time you lift the lid, heat escapes, and it prolongs the cooking time.

Resist the temptation to check on your dish frequently. Trust the slow-cooking process, and only open the lid when necessary.

- Utilize the Keep Warm Function:

After your food has finished cooking, take advantage of the Crock Pot's Keep Warm function. This feature automatically shifts the slow cooker to a low temperature to keep your food warm for up to 6 hours. It's especially useful when your meal is ready before serving time.

- Adjust Seasoning at the End:

Flavors can intensify during the slow-cooking process. Therefore, it's often a good idea to adjust seasoning towards the end of the cooking time. Taste your dish and add more salt, pepper, herbs, or spices if necessary.

- Cleaning and Maintenance:

Ensure the longevity of your Crock Pot by following proper cleaning and maintenance practices. The removable stoneware and lid are dishwasher safe, making cleanup a breeze. Regularly check the rubber gasket and locking mechanism for any signs of wear or damage to maintain an airtight seal.

- Adapt Recipes for Slow Cooking:

  While many recipes can be adapted for slow cooking, it's essential to recognize that not all dishes are suitable. Slow cooking works best with recipes that involve braising, simmering, or stewing. Adjust cooking times and liquid levels accordingly when adapting recipes.

- Experiment with Flavors:

  Slow cooking allows flavors to develop and meld together over time. Don't hesitate to experiment with different herbs, spices, and seasonings to tailor the dish to your taste. Keep notes on successful combinations for future reference.

- Use a Meat Thermometer:

  For dishes involving meats, use a meat thermometer to ensure they reach a safe internal temperature. This is especially important for larger cuts of meat. The programmable nature of the Crock Pot allows you to set precise cooking times, but checking the internal temperature provides an extra layer of assurance.

- Plan for Thicker Sauces:

  Slow cooking tends to produce thicker sauces due to reduced evaporation. If you prefer a thinner consistency, you may need to adjust the amount of liquid in your recipes or dilute the sauce towards the end of the cooking process.

- Invest in Quality Ingredients:

  Slow cooking accentuates the flavors of your ingredients. Therefore, using high-quality, fresh ingredients can make a significant difference in the final taste of your dish. Choose fresh produce, quality meats, and flavorful broths for the best results.

In summary, successful Crock-Pot cooking is a combination of thoughtful preparation, proper layering, attention to liquid levels, patience, and experimentation with flavors. By following these crucial tips, you can make the most of your programmable slow cooker and create delicious, hassle-free meals for various occasions. Remember that slow cooking is a versatile and forgiving method, allowing you to adapt recipes to your preferences while enjoying the convenience of this popular kitchen appliance.

How to Take Care of the Slow Cooker

Taking proper care of your Crock Pot Programmable Cook & Carry Slow Cooker with Digital Timer is essential to ensure its longevity and optimal performance. Here are some guidelines to help you maintain and care for your slow cooker:

Cleaning:

Removable Parts: The removable stoneware, glass lid, and locking gasket are usually dishwasher safe. Always refer to the specific model's user manual for confirmation. If dishwasher safe, place these components in the dishwasher for easy cleaning.

Base Unit: Wipe down the base unit with a damp cloth. Make sure to unplug the unit before cleaning. Never immerse the base in water or any liquid to prevent electrical damage.

Storing:

Lid and Gasket: Store the lid separately from the base to avoid any odor transfer. Ensure that the rubber gasket is clean and dry before storing to prevent mold or mildew growth.

Cord Storage: Some models come with cord storage features. Utilize these to keep the cord neatly stored and prevent any damage.

Handling:

Lid and Stoneware: Handle the glass lid and stoneware with care, as they can be fragile. Avoid sudden temperature changes, such as placing hot stoneware on a cold surface or vice versa, to prevent cracking.

Transporting: Utilize the secure locking lid and rubber gasket when transporting the slow cooker. This ensures an airtight seal, preventing spills and messes during transit.

Temperature Settings:

Avoid Abrupt Temperature Changes: When transitioning between temperature settings (High, Low, Warm), it's advisable to allow a few minutes for the slow cooker to adjust gradually. Abrupt changes may affect the cooking process.

Timer and Auto-Warm Feature:

Proper Usage: Follow the recommended cooking times provided in the recipe book or user manual. Utilize the digital timer for precise cooking durations. The auto-warm feature is convenient for keeping your food warm after cooking without overcooking.

Regular Maintenance:

Inspect for Wear: Periodically check the condition of the gasket, lid, and other components. If you notice any signs of wear, such as cracks or tears, replace the affected parts promptly to maintain the slow cooker's performance.

Avoiding Sharp Objects:

Utensils: Use utensils that are gentle on the stoneware to avoid scratching. Sharp objects can damage the non-stick coating and affect the longevity of the slow cooker.

Storage Environment:

Dry Storage: Store the slow cooker in a cool, dry place. Avoid storing it in areas with extreme temperatures or humidity, as these conditions can affect the electronic components over time.

By following these care guidelines, you can ensure that your Crock Pot Programmable Cook & Carry Slow Cooker remains in excellent condition, providing you with delicious meals for many years to come.

Chapter 1: Breakfast and Brunch

Crock Pot Breakfast Avocado Toast

Prep Time: 15 Mins   Cook Time: 2 Hours   Serves: 4

Ingredients:

- 4 slices of bread
- 2 ripe avocados, mashed
- 4 large eggs
- 1 cup diced tomatoes
- 1/2 cup crumbled cooked bacon
- Salt and pepper to taste
- Chopped fresh parsley for garnish (optional)

Directions:

1. Place a slice of bread in each quadrant of a greased crock pot.
2. Spread mashed avocado on each slice of bread.
3. Make a well in the center of each avocado toast and crack an egg into it.
4. Sprinkle diced tomatoes and crumbled cooked bacon over the top.
5. Season with salt and pepper.
6. Cover and cook on low for 2 hours, or until the eggs are set and the bread is toasted.
7. Garnish with chopped fresh parsley if desired.

Nutritional Value (Amount per Serving):

Calories: 341; Fat: 25.44; Carb: 23.67; Protein: 9.4

Scrambled Tofu Breakfast Burrito

Prep Time: 10 Mins   Cook Time: 8 Hours   Serves: 2

Ingredients:

- 1 1/2 cups black beans, rinsed and drained
- 7 ounces tofu, crumbled
- 2 tablespoons cooked onion
- 2 tablespoons green pepper, minced
- 3/4 cup water
- 1/2 teaspoon ground turmeric
- 1/4 teaspoon ground cumin
- 1/4 teaspoon chili powder
- 1/4 teaspoon smoked paprika
- Salt and pepper, to taste
- 4 whole-wheat burrito-sized tortillas, use gluten-free

Directions:

1. The night before: Add black beans andsmoked paprika, and cook on low for 7 to 9 hours.
2. In the morning: Taste and add salt and pepper. If your tortillas are stiff, put them one at a time over the mixture in the slow cooker, and steam them into submission.
3. Spoon ¼ of the mixture onto the tortillas.
4. Add any extras you'd like, roll up, and serve.

Nutritional Value (Amount per Serving):

Calories: 1056; Fat: 30.44; Carb: 147.15; Protein: 58.04

Crock Pot Breakfast Grits

Prep Time: 10 Mins   Cook Time: 3 Hours   Serves: 4

Ingredients:

- 1 cup stone-ground grits
- 4 cups water
- 1 cup milk
- 1/4 cup unsalted butter
- 1 cup shredded cheddar cheese
- Salt and pepper to taste
- Cooked bacon or sausage for topping (optional)

Directions:

1. In the crock pot, combine grits, water, milk, and unsalted butter.
2. Stir well.
3. Cover and cook on low for 3 hours, stirring occasionally, until the grits are creamy and tender.
4. Stir in shredded cheddar cheese until melted.
5. Season with salt and pepper.
6. Serve hot, topped with cooked bacon or sausage if desired.

Nutritional Value (Amount per Serving):

Calories: 475; Fat: 40.18; Carb: 20.51; Protein: 14.43

Kefir Yogurt

Prep Time: 10 Mins   Cook Time: 4 Hours 5 Mins   Serves: 8

Ingredients:

- 4 cups milk
- ¼ cup instant nonfat dry milk powder, or more to taste
- ½ cup plain kefir

Directions:

1. Preheat a slow cooker on Low.
2. Whisk milk and dry milk powder together in a saucepan over medium heat until almost boiling, about 4 minutes. Cool milk to lukewarm.
3. Gently stir kefir into milk mixture until just blended. Pour mixture into yogurt containers or slow cooker.

4. Cook on Low until desired level of tartness and yogurt consistency is reached, 4 to 10 hours. Chill yogurt in the refrigerator, at least 2 hours.

Nutritional Value (Amount per Serving):

Calories: 178; Fat: 12.68; Carb: 9.88; Protein: 7.86

Slow Cooker Warm Berry Compote

Prep Time: 5 Mins   Cook Time: 2 Hours   Serves: 8

Ingredients:

- 6 cups frozen mixed berries
- 1/2 cup granulated sugar
- Zest and juice of one medium orange
- 2 tablespoons cornstarch
- 2 tablespoons water

Directions:

1. Lightly grease a slow cooker. Add berries, sugar, orange juice and zest and stir to combine.
2. Cover and cook on low until bubbling, about 2 hours.
3. In a small bowl, stir together cornstarch and water. Whisk into berry mixture and mix well. Cover and cook another 10-15 minutes, or until mixture is thickened.
4. Serve warm or at room temperature.

Nutritional Value (Amount per Serving):

Calories: 144; Fat: 3; Carb: 25.65; Protein: 3.77

Slow-Cooker Stone-Ground Grits

Prep Time: 10 Mins   Cook Time: 3 Hours   Serves: 6

Ingredients:

- 8 large eggs
- 1/2 cup milk
- 1 cup smoked salmon, flaked
- 1/4 cup diced red onions
- 1/4 cup capers
- 1/4 cup cream cheese, diced
- Salt and pepper to taste
- Fresh dill for garnish (optional)

Directions:

1. Stir together grits and water in a slow cooker. Let stand 2 minutes, allowing grits to settle to bottom; tilt slow cooker slightly, and skim off solids using a fine wire-mesh strainer. Cover and cook on HIGH 2 1/2 to 3 hours or until grits are creamy and tender, stirring every 45 minutes. Season with salt and freshly ground pepper to taste.

Calories: 226; Fat: 14.55; Carb: 3.31; Protein: 19.5

Crock Pot Breakfast Quinoa with Mixed Berries

Prep Time: 15 Mins   Cook Time: 2 Hours 30 Mins   Serves: 4

Ingredients:

- 1 cup quinoa, rinsed and drained
- 2 cups almond milk (or any milk of your choice)
- 1/4 cup honey or maple syrup
- 1 tsp vanilla extract
- 1/2 tsp ground cinnamon
- 1 cup mixed berries (e.g., strawberries, blueberries, raspberries)
- Sliced almonds for garnish (optional)

Directions:

1. In the greased crock pot, combine quinoa, almond milk, honey (or maple syrup), vanilla extract, and ground cinnamon.
2. Stir well.
3. Cover and cook on low for 2.5 hours, stirring occasionally, until the quinoa is tender and the mixture is creamy.
4. About 15 minutes before serving, gently fold in the mixed berries.
5. Cover and continue to cook until the berries are heated through.
6. Serve hot, garnished with sliced almonds if desired.

Nutritional Value (Amount per Serving):

Calories: 293; Fat: 4.49; Carb: 56.91; Protein: 7

Mals Maple Date Pecan Granola

Prep Time: 5 Mins   Cook Time: 3 Hours   Serves: 6

Ingredients:

- 6 tablespoons applesauce
- ¼ cup pure maple syrup
- 2 tablespoons brown sugar (Optional)
- 1 teaspoon ground cinnamon
- ¼ teaspoon salt
- ¼ teaspoon vanilla extract
- ¼ teaspoon maple extract
- 1 tablespoon hemp seed hearts (Optional)
- 1 tablespoon chia seeds (Optional)

- 3 cups rolled oats
- 1 cup chopped pecans
- 1 cup Medjool dates, pitted and chopped

Directions:

1. Pour applesauce, maple syrup, brown sugar, cinnamon, salt, vanilla and maple extracts, hemp hearts, and chia seeds into a slow cooker. Stir until well combined; add oats and pecans and stir again.
2. Cook the granola in the slow cooker on high for 3 hours, venting the lid slightly. If you smell the granola cooking, it's time to stir. Keep an eye on it or it will burn if not stirred occasionally.
3. Pour the finished granola onto a baking sheet lined with parchment paper and allow to cool completely. Store in an airtight container and enjoy!

Nutritional Value (Amount per Serving):

Calories: 311; Fat: 16.68; Carb: 50.53; Protein: 10.59

Crock Pot Breakfast Bacon Tater

Prep Time: 15 Mins   Cook Time: 7 Hours   Serves: 6-8

Ingredients:

- 1 pound package frozen tater tot potatoes
- 1/2 pound diced Canadian bacon
- 2 onions, chopped
- 1-1/2 cups shredded Cheddar cheese
- 1/4 cup grated Parmesan cheese
- 6 eggs
- 1/2 cup whole milk
- 2 tablespoons flour
- salt and pepper to taste

Directions:

1. Gather the ingredients.
2. In a crock pot, layer the ingredients in order: one third of the tater tots, bacon, onions, and cheeses.
3. Repeat layers two more times, ending with cheeses.
4. In a medium mixing bowl, combine eggs, milk, and flour and beat with whisk or egg beater until combined.
5. Season with salt and pepper to taste.
6. Pour this mixture over the layers in the crock pot.
7. Cover the crockpot and cook on low for 6-8 hours or until an instant read thermometer measures at least 160°F.

Nutritional Value (Amount per Serving):

Calories: 255; Fat: 11.01; Carb: 20.84; Protein: 18.09

Slow-Cooker Butternut Squash Shakshuka

Prep Time:10 Mins   Cook Time: 11 Hours 25 Mins   Serves: 6

Ingredients:

- 3/4 cup chopped red sweet pepper
- 1 small onion, halved and thinly sliced
- 1 medium fresh jalapeño pepper, seeded and finely chopped
- 2 cloves garlic, minced
- 1 teaspoon dried oregano, crushed
- 1 teaspoon ground cumin
- 1/2 teaspoon salt
- 1/2 teaspoon black pepper
- 2 pounds butternut squash, peeled, seeded, and chopped (6 cups)
- 1 (15-ounce) can crushed tomatoes
- 1 (8-ounce) can tomato sauce
- 6 eggs
- 3/4 cup crumbled feta cheese (3 ounces)
- 2 tablespoons snipped fresh Italian parsley
- Pita bread rounds, warmed

Directions:

1. In a slow cooker, combine first eight ingredients (toblack pepper).
2. Stir in squash, crushed tomatoes, and tomato sauce.
3. Cover and cook on low 11 to 12 hours or high 5½ to 6 hours.
4. Break an egg into a custard cup. Make an indentation in squash mixture; slide egg into indentation.
5. Repeat with remaining eggs. Cover and cook 25 to 35 more minutes or until eggs are desired doneness.
6. Top servings with cheese and parsley.
7. Serve with pita bread.

Nutritional Value (Amount per Serving):

Calories: 282; Fat: 14.09; Carb: 26.69; Protein: 14.44

Slow Cooker Mocha

Prep Time: 10 Mins   Cook Time: 2 Hours   Serves: 4

Ingredients:

- 3 cups strong brewed coffee
- ⅓cup Unsweetened cocoa powder put through a sieve to get out lumps
- ¾ cup coconut sugar

- 1 ¾ cups almond milk
- 1 teaspoon vanilla extract

Directions:

1. Mix well the brewed coffee, almond milk, cocoa powder, coconut sugar, and vanilla extract.
2. Turn to high and let cook for 2 hours.
3. Stir again and serve in mugs.
4. Makes 36 ounces which is a little bit more than 4 cups.
5. It is easy to double or triple for a larger group. Just make sure your pot is large enough.

Nutritional Value (Amount per Serving):

Calories: 137; Fat: 1.67; Carb: 29.04; Protein: 1.45

Crock Pot Sausage Mediterranean Quiche

Prep Time: 10 Mins   Cook Time: 3 Hours   Serves: 6

Ingredients:

- 6 egg whites
- 2 eggs
- 1 cup skim milk
- 1 cup Heart Healthy Bisquick
- 2 cup chopped spinach
- 1 cup Feta with Italian herbs
- 1 tsp minced garlic
- 1/2 cup julienne cut sun-dried tomatoes, drained
- 1/2 cup shredded mozzarella cheese
- 1 package Jones Dairy Farm Sausage Links (10 links), chopped
- salt and pepper to taste
- chopped basil for garnish

Directions:

1. Spray a slow cooker with cooking spray or olive oil.
2. In a large bowl, whisk together eggs, eggwhites, bisquick, and milk. Pour into slow cooker.
3. Add spinach, feta, mozzarella, tomatoes, garlic and sausage; stir well.
4. Cook covered on high heat setting for 3 hours or on low setting for approximately 5½ hours.
5. The quiche is done when the sides are browned and the middle is fluffy and cooked through.
6. Slice and serve, garnished with basil and additional feta. Enjoy!

Crock Pot Breakfast Crepes

Prep Time: 20 Mins   Cook Time: 3 Hours   Serves: 4

Ingredients:

- 1 cup all-purpose flour
- 2 large eggs
- 1 1/2 cups milk
- 2 tbsp sugar
- 1/2 tsp vanilla extract
- Pinch of salt
- Butter for greasing
- Fresh fruit, Nutella, or whipped cream for filling

Directions:

1. In a blender, combine the flour, eggs, milk, sugar, vanilla extract, and a pinch of salt. Blend until smooth.
2. Grease the crock pot with butter.
3. Pour a small amount of batter into the crock pot and swirl it around to coat the bottom thinly.
4. Cook on low for about 2 minutes or until set.
5. Carefully remove the crepe and repeat the process with the remaining batter.
6. Serve the crepes with your choice of fillings, such as fresh fruit, Nutella, or whipped cream.

Nutritional Value (Amount per Serving):

Calories: 281; Fat: 8.78; Carb: 44.31; Protein: 7.71

Chapter 2: Stews and Soups

Slow Cooker King Ranch Chicken Soup

Prep Time: 25 Mins   Cook Time: 4 Hours   Serves: 6

Ingredients:

- 8 tbsp butter
- 2 cloves garlic minced
- 1/2 c. all-purpose flour
- 3 c. low-sodium chicken broth
- 4 tsp chili powder
- 1 tbsp ground cumin
- 1 tbsp garlic powder
- 1 tsp salt
- Freshly ground pepper to taste
- 1 1/2 lb boneless skinless chicken breasts
- 1 10 oz can diced tomatoes with green chilies (mild, original or hot depending on your heat preference)
- 1 medium jalapeno minced (seeds and membranes left intact for spicy, removed for mild)
- 2 c. Colby Jack cheese, plus more for topping
- Tortilla chips for servings,
- Fresh cilantro chopped, for serving, optional

Directions:

1. Melt the butter in a medium saucepan over medium-low heat. Add the garlic and saute until it is fragrant and light golden brown, about 1 minutes.
2. Stir in flour and whisk continuously for 1 minute. Slowly whisk in the chicken broth. Increase the heat to a simmer and whisk continuously for several minutes, until the sauce is smooth and thickened. Remove saucepan from heat, and stir in chili powder, cumin, garlic powder and salt. Add black pepper to taste and set sauce aside.
3. Place the chicken breasts in a large slow cooker. Top them with the diced tomatoes with green chilies and jalapeno. Pour the sauce over the top. Cover slow cooker and cook on low for 4- hours, until chicken is tender and cooked through, but not overcooked.
4. Transfer chicken to cutting board, stir cheese into the slow cooker and cover the slow cooker while you prepare chicken. Pull chicken into large chunks and stir in back into the slow cooker.
5. Cover the slow cooker and cook for 15 minutes, until the cheese is melted and the ingredients are heated through. Stir well.
6. To serve, crush tortilla chips into a bowl and ladle the soup over the top. Garnish with extra cheese and cilantro, if desired.

Calories: 747; Fat: 45.38; Carb: 15.02; Protein: 69.31

Sirloin Burger Soup

Prep Time: 20 Mins   Cook Time: 5 Hours   Serves: 4

Ingredients:

- 1 1/2 cups beef broth
- 1 (10 1/2-ounce) can condensed beef broth
- 1 (14 1/2-ounce) can diced tomatoes, diced
- 3/4 cup carrots, coarsely chopped
- 1 cup onion, chopped
- 1/2 to 1 cup celery, thinly sliced
- 1 1/2 cups large potato, cut into small cubes
- 1/4 teaspoon freshly ground black pepper
- 10 ounces lean ground beef, formed into 2 to 3 patties
- 2 tablespoons oil, as needed
- 1/4 cup frozen peas, optional
- 1/4 cup frozen corn, optional
- 1 tablespoon parsley, freshly chopped, for garnish

Directions:

1. In a crock pot, combine beef broth and condensed broth with tomatoes, chopped carrots, onion, celery, and potato. Add a little pepper. Cover and cook on high for 3 hours, until vegetables are tender.
2. Cook the burgers in a grill pan, on charcoal or gas grill, in a skillet or under a broiler, using a little oil in the pan or broiler rack.
3. Cut cooked burgers into small pieces and add to the soup. Add peas and corn, if using. Cook on low for about 2 hours longer. Garnish with fresh chopped parsley and serve.

Nutritional Value (Amount per Serving):

Calories: 425; Fat: 20.6; Carb: 32.32; Protein: 28.03

Mediterranean Lentil Stew

Prep Time: 20 Mins   Cook Time: 3 Hours 10 Mins   Serves: 10

Ingredients:

- 5 cups water
- 2 ½ cubes vegetable bouillon, or more to taste

- 2 cups dry lentils
- 5 small carrots, peeled and diced
- 2 medium potatoes, peeled and diced
- 3 teaspoons ground cumin, or to taste
- 1 teaspoon ground coriander
- 1 tablespoon olive oil
- 1 small onion, diced
- 4 cloves garlic, minced
- ½ (6 ounce) can tomato paste, or to taste
- ½ teaspoon sea salt, or to taste
- ½ teaspoon freshly ground black pepper, or to taste
- ½ (8 ounce) package fresh spinach, torn

Directions:

1. Warm water and vegetable bouillon in a slow cooker on High until dissolved. Add lentils, carrots, and potatoes.
2. Heat a medium saucepan over medium heat. Add cumin and coriander, and cook and stir until fragrant, about 20 seconds. Add oil, followed by onion. Cook, stirring occasionally, 2 to 3 minutes. Add garlic and saute for 30 seconds. Remove from heat and transfer to the slow cooker. Stir. Add tomato paste, salt, and pepper. Stir in spinach.
3. Cook on High, stirring every 30 minutes, until lentils are tender and stew has thickened, 3 to 4 hours.

Nutritional Value (Amount per Serving):

Calories: 260; Fat: 8.11; Carb: 36.73; Protein: 11.61

Irish Potato Leek Soup

Prep Time: 20 Mins   Cook Time: 6 Hours   Serves: 6

Ingredients:

- 4 cups potatoes, peeled and diced
- 3 leeks, cleaned and sliced
- 1 onion, chopped
- 2 cloves of garlic, minced
- 4 cups vegetable broth
- 1 cup heavy cream
- 1/4 cup unsalted butter
- Salt and pepper to taste
- Chopped fresh chives for garnish (optional)

Directions:

1. Place diced potatoes, sliced leeks, chopped onion, minced garlic, vegetable broth, and butter in the crock pot.
2. Cover and cook on low for 6 hours.
3. Use an immersion blender to blend the soup until smooth.
4. Stir in heavy cream, salt, and pepper.

5. Serve hot, garnished with chopped fresh chives if desired.

Calories: 239; Fat: 12.81; Carb: 29.09; Protein: 3.83

New England Clam Chowder

Prep Time: 10 Mins   Cook Time: 6 Hours   Serves: 6

Ingredients:

- 3 cans (10 oz each) minced clams, drained, juice reserved
- 4 cups diced potatoes
- 2 onions, chopped
- 4 slices bacon, cooked and crumbled
- 2 cups half-and-half
- 4 cups chicken broth
- 2 bay leaves
- Salt and pepper to taste
- Chopped fresh parsley for garnish (optional)

Directions:

1. Place diced potatoes, chopped onions, crumbled bacon, half-and-half, chicken broth, reserved clam juice, bay leaves, salt, and pepper in the crock pot.
2. Cover and cook on low for 6 hours.
3. Stir in minced clams and let it heat through for another 15 minutes.
4. Remove the bay leaves before serving.
5. Serve hot, garnished with chopped fresh parsley if desired.

Nutritional Value (Amount per Serving):

Calories: 508; Fat: 19.36; Carb: 39.81; Protein: 42.14

Slow Cooker Navy Bean Soup with Ham

Prep Time: 15 Mins   Cook Time: 10 Hours   Serves: 6

Ingredients:

- 1 pound dry navy beans, soak overnight following package directions
- 1 large carrot, finely chopped
- 1 cup finely chopped celery, including some leaves
- 1 medium onion, chopped
- 1 to 1 1/2 pounds ham hocks, or a meaty ham bone
- 1 teaspoon salt, or to taste

- Freshly ground black pepper, to taste

Directions:

1. Gather the ingredients.
2. Drain the beans thoroughly and put them in a stock pot and cover with about 6 cups of fresh water. Bring to a boil over high heat. Reduce the heat to the lowest setting and simmer for about 30 minutes.
3. Put the beans and cooking water in the slow cooker with the diced carrot, celery, onion, and ham or ham bone. Cover and cook on low for 6 to 9 hours, or until the beans are tender.
4. Remove the ham hock or ham bone and discard skin, fat, and bone. Cut the meat into small pieces and then return to the soup. Ladle the hot soup into bowls.
5. The beans can be mashed or partially mashed to thicken the soup if desired.

Nutritional Value (Amount per Serving):

Calories: 264; Fat: 13.83; Carb: 7.36; Protein: 27.45

Minestrone Soup

Prep Time: 10 Mins   Cook Time: 4 Hours 30 Mins   Serves: 6

Ingredients:

- 2 cans diced tomatoes, 14.5 oz cans
- 3 tbsp tomato paste
- 1/4 cup Parmesan cheese
- 4 cups vegetable broth, or chicken broth
- 2 cups water
- 1 cup carrots, diced
- 1 cup celery, diced
- 1.5 cups onion, diced
- 4 cloves garlic, finely minced
- 1 tbsp ginger, freshly grated
- 1 tsp oregano, dried
- 1 cup zucchini, diced
- 1.5 cups tubular pasta
- 2 cups spinach, roughly chopped
- 1 cup green beans, frozen
- 1 sprig rosemary, fresh
- 1 tbsp Italian seasoning
- 1 Bay leaf
- Salt and pepper

- 1 can red kidney beans, 15 oz. can, drained and rinsed

Directions:

1. In a slow cooker, add diced tomatoes, tomato paste, Parmesan cheese, vegetable broth, water, carrots, celery, onions, garlic, ginger, oregano, rosemary, Italian seasoning, bay leaf, salt and pepper.
2. Cook on Low heat for 6-8 hours onHigh heat for 3-4 hours.
3. Add red kidney beans, Northern beans, zucchini, pasta and cook on High heat for an additional 20- 25 minutes until pasta is tender.
4. Stir in the spinach, green beans and cook for an additional 10 minutes until cooked through. Enjoy!

Nutritional Value (Amount per Serving):

Calories: 130; Fat: 2.1; Carb: 25.05; Protein: 4.51

Slow Cooker Polish Sausage and Cabbage Soup

Prep Time: 20 Mins   Cook Time: 7 Hours 20 Mins   Serves: 6

Ingredients:

- 1 to 1 1/2 pounds red-skinned or round white potatoes
- 1 to 1 1/2 pounds Polish kielbasa sausage
- 1 large onion, chopped
- 1/2 medium head cabbage, shredded or chopped
- 1 quart low-sodium or unsalted chicken stock
- 1 (14 1/2-ounce) can diced tomatoes, optional
- Kosher salt, to taste
- Freshly ground black pepper, to taste
- 4 to 6 strips bacon, diced, optional
- 1/2 teaspoon caraway seeds

Directions:

1. Gather ingredients.
2. Dice the potatoes (peeled or not) into 1/2-inch cubes. Put the potatoes in the slow cooker.
3. Dice the sausage into 1/2-inch cubes.
4. Place a large skillet over medium heat. Add the diced bacon, if using, and cook until crisp. Drain on paper towels and then add to the slow cooker.
5. Wipe the skillet out and place it over medium-high heat. Add the diced sausage and onion. Cook while frequently stirring until the sausage and onions have browned. Drain well and transfer to the slow cooker with the potatoes.
6. Add 2 tablespoons of butter to the skillet along with the cabbage and place it back over medium-high heat. Cook while frequently stirring until the

cabbage begins to brown. Transfer to the slow cooker.

7. Add the chicken stock to the slow cooker along with the tomatoes and caraway seeds if using.
8. Cover and cook on low for 7 to 9 hours.
9. Taste and add salt and pepper, as needed. Serve the soup with crusty bread.

Nutritional Value (Amount per Serving):

Calories: 516; Fat: 31.65; Carb: 28.28; Protein: 33.85

Tortellini Soup

Prep Time: 20 Mins   Cook Time: 6 Hours   Serves: 6

Ingredients:

- 1 pound Italian sausage, casings removed and crumbled
- 2 cans (14 oz each) diced tomatoes
- 1 onion, chopped
- 2 carrots, sliced
- 2 celery stalks, chopped
- 4 cups chicken broth
- 2 teaspoons dried basil
- 1 teaspoon dried oregano
- Salt and pepper to taste
- 1 package (9 oz) cheese tortellini
- Fresh basil leaves for garnish (optional)

Directions:

1. In a skillet, brown the crumbled Italian sausage over medium heat. Drain excess fat.
2. Place browned sausage, diced tomatoes, chopped onion, sliced carrots, chopped celery, chicken broth, dried basil, dried oregano, salt, and pepper in the crock pot.
3. Cover and cook on low for 6 hours.
4. Stir in cheese tortellini and let it cook for an additional 15 minutes.
5. Serve hot, garnished with fresh basil leaves if desired.

Nutritional Value (Amount per Serving):

Calories: 643; Fat: 43.56; Carb: 7.03; Protein: 53.26

Moroccan Lamb Stew

Prep Time: 20 Mins   Cook Time: 8 Hours   Serves: 6

Ingredients:

- 2 pounds boneless lamb shoulder, cut into chunks
- 2 onions, chopped
- 3 cloves of garlic, minced
- 2 carrots, sliced
- 2 potatoes, peeled and diced
- 1 can (14 oz) diced tomatoes
- 1 can (14 oz) chickpeas, drained and rinsed
- 4 cups beef or lamb broth
- 2 teaspoons ground cumin
- 1 teaspoon ground coriander
- 1 teaspoon ground cinnamon
- 1/2 teaspoon ground ginger
- Salt and pepper to taste
- Chopped fresh cilantro for garnish (optional)
- Cooked couscous or rice for serving

Directions:

1. In a large bowl, season the lamb chunks with salt, pepper, ground cumin, ground coriander, ground cinnamon, and ground ginger.
2. Place the seasoned lamb, chopped onions, minced garlic, sliced carrots, diced potatoes, diced tomatoes, chickpeas, beef or lamb broth, salt, and pepper in the crock pot.
3. Cover and cook on low for 8 hours.
4. Serve hot over cooked couscous or rice, garnished with chopped fresh cilantro if desired.

Nutritional Value (Amount per Serving):

Calories: 481; Fat: 15.89; Carb: 38.22; Protein: 47.67

Slow Cooker Greek Lemon Chicken Soup

Prep Time: 15 Mins   Cook Time: 4 Hours   Serves: 6

Ingredients:

- 1 lb. boneless skinless chicken breast
- 1 yellow onion chopped
- 1 large stalk celery chopped
- 1 clove garlic minced
- 4 cups chicken stock homemade or low sodium
- 2 cups water or sub with more chicken stock for added flavor
- 1/2 cup uncooked white rice or orzo pasta do not use instant rice
- ¼ cup fresh lemon juice

- 2 large eggs
- salt and pepper to taste

Directions:

1. Season the chicken with salt and pepper. Place the chicken, onion, celery, garlic, stock and water in your slow cooker. Cook about 3 hours on high, or 4-5 hours on low, adding the rice or orzo during the last hour or so of cooking time to prevent overcooking.
2. When the chicken is done, remove it from the slow cooker and allow to cool slightly. Chop into chunks or shred, and place back in the slow cooker.
3. Place the eggs in a medium bowl and beat lightly, then whisk in the lemon juice until combined. Place about 1 cup of hot soup broth in a measuring cup, and add a few droplets at a time to the egg-lemon mixture whisking constantly to temper the eggs. Continue adding the hot broth in a slow, steady stream while whisking constantly.
4. After all the stock has been added, add the egg-lemon mixture to the soup in the slow cooker and stir to combine. Season with salt and pepper to taste, serve, and enjoy!

Nutritional Value (Amount per Serving):

Calories: 180; Fat: 5.44; Carb: 13.24; Protein: 19.48

Tuscan White Bean and Kale Soup

Prep Time: 20 Mins   Cook Time: 6 Hours   Serves: 6

Ingredients:

- 2 cans (15 oz each) cannellini beans, drained and rinsed
- 1 bunch kale, stems removed and leaves chopped
- 1 onion, chopped
- 2 cloves of garlic, minced
- 4 cups vegetable broth
- 1 can (14 oz) diced tomatoes
- 1 teaspoon dried rosemary
- 1 teaspoon dried thyme
- Salt and pepper to taste
- Grated Parmesan cheese for garnish (optional)

Directions:

1. Place cannellini beans, chopped kale, chopped onion, minced garlic, vegetable broth, diced tomatoes, dried rosemary, dried thyme, salt, and pepper in the crock pot.
2. Cover and cook on low for 6 hours.
3. Serve hot, garnished with grated Parmesan cheese if desired.

Nutritional Value (Amount per Serving):

Calories: 150; Fat: 2.36; Carb: 26.59; Protein: 7.45

Chapter 3: Poultry

Slow Cooker French Wine and Mustard Chicken

Prep Time: 10 Mins   Cook Time: 5 Hours   Serves: 6

Ingredients:

- 1 cup dry white wine
- 1/3 cup heavy cream or canned full fat coconut milk
- 2 tablespoons dijon mustard
- 2 tablespoons grainy dijon mustard
- 2 shallots chopped
- 2 cloves garlic, minced or grated
- kosher salt and pepper
- 2 pounds boneless chicken breasts, skin on or off
- 1 tablespoon extra virgin olive oil
- 2 tablespoons fresh thyme leaves
- 1 tablespoon fresh chopped sage
- 2 tablespoons salted butter
- 1/3 cup freshly grated Parmesan cheese
- 1/2 bunch kale, chopped
- mashed potatoes or steamed rice, for serving

Directions:

1. In the bowl of your slow cooker, combine the wine, milk/cream, both mustards, shallots, garlic, and a pinch each of salt and pepper.
2. Rub the chicken with thyme, sage, and a pinch each of salt and pepper. Heat the olive oil in a large skillet over medium high heat. When the oil shimmers, add the chicken and sear until golden brown on both sides, about 3 minutes per side. Remove the chicken from the skillet and place directly into the slow cooker, skin side up, along with any juices left in the skillet. Add the butter.
3. Cover the slow cooker and cook on low for 4-6 hours or on high for 2-3 hours. During the last 30 minutes of cooking, add the Parmesan and kale, gently tossing to combine.
4. Serve the chicken over mashed potatoes or rice and spoon the creamy mustard sauce over top the chicken. Serve with additional herbs and Parmesan.

Nutritional Value (Amount per Serving):

Calories: 361; Fat: 16.13; Carb: 11.1; Protein: 41.61

Slow Cooker Cranberry Chicken

Prep Time: 5 Mins   Cook Time: 4 Hours   Serves: 4

Ingredients:

- 4 skinless, boneless chicken breast halves
- 1 (16 ounce) bottle Catalina salad dressing
- 1 (14.5 ounce) can whole berry cranberry sauce
- 1 envelope onion soup mix

Directions:

1. Place the chicken breasts in the bottom of a slow cooker. Pour the salad dressing, cranberry sauce, and onion soup mix over the chicken.
2. Cook on Low 4 to 6 hours.

Nutritional Value (Amount per Serving):

Calories: 220; Fat: 2; Carb: 55.4; Protein: 3.02

Crock Pot Chicken and Sausage Gumbo

Prep Time: 20 Mins   Cook Time: 6 Hours   Serves: 6

Ingredients:

- 4 boneless, skinless chicken thighs, cut into bite-sized pieces
- 1 lb Andouille sausage, sliced
- 1 onion, chopped
- 1 green bell pepper, chopped
- 1 red bell pepper, chopped
- 3 stalks celery, chopped
- 4 cloves garlic, minced
- 1 can (14 oz) diced tomatoes
- 4 cups chicken broth
- 2 teaspoons gumbo file powder (optional)
- 1 teaspoon dried thyme
- 1 teaspoon paprika
- 1/2 teaspoon cayenne pepper (adjust to taste)
- Salt and pepper to taste
- Cooked white rice for serving
- Chopped green onions for garnish (optional)

Directions:

1. Place chicken pieces, sliced Andouille sausage, chopped onion, chopped green bell pepper, chopped red bell pepper, chopped celery, minced garlic, diced tomatoes, chicken broth, gumbo file powder (if using), dried thyme, paprika, cayenne pepper, salt, and pepper in the crock pot.
2. Cover and cook on low for 6 hours.
3. Serve the chicken and sausage gumbo over cooked white rice.

4. Garnish with chopped green onions if desired.

Nutritional Value (Amount per Serving):

Calories: 1078; Fat: 44.22; Carb: 89.52; Protein: 81.29

Crock Pot Chicken and Eggplant Parmesan

Prep Time: 20 Mins   Cook Time: 4 Hours   Serves: 4

Ingredients:

- 4 boneless, skinless chicken breasts
- 1 eggplant, sliced into rounds
- 1 cup marinara sauce
- 1 cup shredded mozzarella cheese
- 1/2 cup grated Parmesan cheese
- 1/2 teaspoon dried basil
- 1/2 teaspoon dried oregano
- Salt and pepper to taste
- Cooked spaghetti for serving
- Chopped fresh basil for garnish (optional)

Directions:

1. Place chicken breasts in the crock pot.
2. Layer eggplant rounds over the chicken.
3. Spread marinara sauce over the eggplant.
4. Sprinkle shredded mozzarella cheese, grated Parmesan cheese, dried basil, dried oregano, salt, and pepper over the top.
5. Cover and cook on low for 4 hours.
6. Serve the chicken and eggplant Parmesan over cooked spaghetti.
7. Garnish with chopped fresh basil if desired.

Nutritional Value (Amount per Serving):

Calories: 1083; Fat: 33.52; Carb: 131.54; Protein: 63.53

Slow Cooker Turkey and Dumplings

Prep Time: 10 Mins   Cook Time: 4 Hours   Serves: 4

Ingredients:

- 2 (10.75 ounce) cans condensed cream of chicken soup
- 1 (15 ounce) can chicken broth
- 1 ½ cups chopped cooked turkey, or more to taste
- 1 cup chopped potatoes, or more to taste

- 1 cup chopped carrots, or more to taste
- ½ onion, chopped
- 2 tablespoons butter
- 1 pinch garlic powder
- 1 pinch poultry seasoning
- ½ (10 ounce) can refrigerated buttermilk biscuit dough, cut into squares

Directions:

1. Mix cream of chicken soup, chicken broth, chopped cooked turkey, potatoes, carrots, onion, butter, garlic powder, and poultry seasoning together in a slow cooker.
2. Cook on High for 3 hours.
3. Stir soup, then arrange biscuits on top. Continue cooking until biscuits are cooked through, about 1 more hour.

Nutritional Value (Amount per Serving):

Calories: 1033; Fat: 83.79; Carb: 26.15; Protein: 41.77

Slow Cooker Yellow Chicken Curry

Prep Time: 15 Mins   Cook Time: 4 Hours   Serves: 4-6

Ingredients:

- 1 medium yellow onion, finely diced or 2 Tbsp dried onion flakes
- 1 lb yellow potatoes (about 3-4 medium potatoes), cubed
- 1 1/2 lbs boneless, skinless chicken thighs, cut into bite size pieces
- 1 (13.5 oz) can full fat coconut milk
- 2 Tbsp brown sugar
- 2 tsp minced garlic
- 1 Tbsp fresh ginger, minced
- 1 tsp ground turmeric
- 1 tsp curry powder
- 1/2 tsp ground coriander seed
- 1 tsp kosher salt
- 1/2 tsp crushed red pepper
- 1 lime, juiced–optional
- Cilantro, for garnish

Directions:

1. In your slow cooker place the onions, potatoes and chicken.
2. In a bowl, stir together the coconut milk, brown sugar, garlic, ginger, turmeric, curry powder, coriander seed, salt and red pepper. Whisk until combined. Pour the mixture over the contents of the slow cooker.
3. Cover and cook on LOW for 4 hours. Test potatoes for tenderness.

4. Gently stir. Stir in the lime juice, if desired. Add in more turmeric and curry powder and salt to taste.
5. Serve curry with cilantro over rice, if desired.

Nutritional Value (Amount per Serving):

Calories: 663; Fat: 33.12; Carb: 73.01; Protein: 20.5

Barbecue Duck Sandwiches

Prep Time: 10 Mins   Cook Time: 8 Hours   Serves: 6

Ingredients:

- 3 lbs duck breast
- 1½ cups ketchup
- ¼ barbecue sauce
- ¼ cup packed brown sugar
- 2 tbsp Worcestershire sauce
- 2 tbsp Dijon mustard
- 1 tsp liquid smoke
- ½ tsp salt
- ¼ tsp garlic powder
- ¼ tsp pepper
- 12 sandwich buns (split)
- Sliced onions, dill pickles, and pickled jalapenos

Directions:

1. Trim pieces of duck breast and place in slow cooker.
2. Place ketchup, barbecue sauce, brown sugar, Worcestershire sauce, Dijon mustard, liquid smoke, salt, garlic powder, and pepper in a slow cooker.
3. Mix sauce and duck breast together.
4. Cook duck breast on low for 8 hours.
5. Using forks, shred duck breast and then remix with sauce.
6. Let reheat for 5 minutes.
7. Serve on sandwich buns with onions, pickles, and jalapenos if desired.
8. Enjoy!

Nutritional Value (Amount per Serving):

Calories: 460; Fat: 13.6; Carb: 34.36; Protein: 49.47

Slow Cooker Chicken and Mushroom Risotto

Prep Time: 15 Mins   Cook Time: 1 Hour 15 Mins   Serves: 6

Ingredients:

- 2 tbs olive oil
- 4 portobello mushrooms, thinly sliced
- 200g button mushrooms, halved
- 50g Coles Australian Salted Butter
- 1 brown onion, finely chopped
- 4 garlic cloves, crushed
- 1 tbsp fresh thyme leaves
- 125ml (1/2 cup) dry white wine
- 1L (4 cups) Massel Chicken Style Liquid Stock
- 440g (2 cups) arborio rice
- 2 cups shredded cooked chicken
- 60g (3/4 cup) finely grated Parmesan cheese

Directions:

1. Heat oil in a large frying pan over medium-high heat. Cook mushrooms, stirring often, for 7-8 minutes or until golden and tender. Transfer to a bowl. Set aside until required.
2. Heat the butter in the same frying pan over medium-high heat until foaming. Add onion, garlic and half the thyme. Cook, stirring, for 5 minutes or until softened. Add the wine and bring to aboil. Add stock and 500ml (2 cups) of water and bring to aboil.
3. Place rice in a slow cooker. Pour over the stock mixture and stir to combine. Cook, covered, on HIGH, for 1 hour or until rice is tender, adding chicken and mushrooms to slow cooker for the last 15 minutes of cooking time. Stir in 40g (1/2 cup) of the Parmesan. Season.
4. Serve the risotto immediately sprinkled with remaining cheese and thyme.

Nutritional Value (Amount per Serving):

Calories: 1013; Fat: 62.08; Carb: 69.98; Protein: 68.77

Slow Cooker Mango Salsa Chicken

Prep Time: 5 Mins   Cook Time: 4-6 Hours   Serves: 8

Ingredients:

- 1/2 cup chicken broth
- 2 pounds boneless skinless chicken thighs or breasts (frozen is okay)
- 1 tbsp soy sauce
- 1 (15 oz) jar Pace's Peach Mango Jalapeno Salsa (or other similar salsa)

Directions:

1. Add chicken broth, chicken, soy sauce and half of the jar of salsa to the

slow cooker.

2. Cover and cook on low for 4-6 hours.
3. Remove the chicken and place on a cutting board. Shred the chicken. If you want to thicken the juices in the slow cooker make a cornstarch slurry by mixing 2 tbsp cornstarch with 2 tbsp water until smooth and then stirring the mixture into the slow cooker on the high setting. Stir the shredded chicken back into the juices in the pot.
4. Stir the remaining half of salsa into the slow cooker.
5. Serve the chicken and sauce with rice, tortillas or even over cauliflower rice.

Nutritional Value (Amount per Serving):

Calories: 167; Fat: 4.37; Carb: 0.99; Protein: 28.9

Crock Pot Chicken Cordon Bleu

Prep Time: 15 Mins   Cook Time: 4 Hours   Serves: 4

Ingredients:

- 4 boneless, skinless chicken breasts
- 4 slices ham
- 4 slices Swiss cheese
- 1 can (10.75 oz) condensed cream of chicken soup
- 1/2 cup chicken broth
- 1 cup bread crumbs
- 1/2 cup melted butter
- Salt and pepper to taste
- Fresh parsley for garnish (optional)

Directions:

1. Place chicken breasts in the crock pot.
2. Top each chicken breast with a slice of ham and a slice of Swiss cheese.
3. In a bowl, mix together condensed cream of chicken soup and chicken broth. Pour the mixture over the chicken.
4. In a separate bowl, combine bread crumbs, melted butter, salt, and pepper. Sprinkle the breadcrumb mixture over the top.
5. Cover and cook on low for 4 hours.
6. Garnish with fresh parsley before serving, if desired.

Nutritional Value (Amount per Serving):

Calories: 1352; Fat: 66.62; Carb: 120.49; Protein: 66.35

Chicken and Cranberry Sauce

Prep Time: 10 Mins   Cook Time: 4 Hours   Serves: 4

Ingredients:

- 4 boneless, skinless chicken thighs
- 1 cup cranberry sauce
- 1/4 cup orange juice
- 2 tablespoons Dijon mustard
- 2 cloves garlic, minced
- 1 teaspoon dried thyme
- Salt and pepper to taste
- Orange zest for garnish (optional)
- Cooked quinoa or rice for serving

Directions:

1. Place chicken thighs in the crock pot.
2. In a bowl, whisk together cranberry sauce, orange juice, Dijon mustard, minced garlic, dried thyme, salt, and pepper.
3. Pour the cranberry sauce mixture over the chicken.
4. Cover and cook on low for 4 hours.
5. Serve the chicken and cranberry sauce over cooked quinoa or rice.
6. Garnish with orange zest if desired.

Nutritional Value (Amount per Serving):

Calories: 1006; Fat: 29.12; Carb: 137.38; Protein: 47.56

Slow Cooker Lemon Artichoke Chicken

Prep Time: 10 Mins   Cook Time: 3 Hours   Serves: 4

Ingredients:

- 2 1/2 to 3 pounds chicken thighs, seasoned with salt pepper
- 30 ounces artichokes
- 1 medium-size onion, sliced
- 1 lemon, sliced
- 1 tbsp oil
- 1/2 cup lemon juice
- 1 /2 cup low-sodium chicken broth
- 1 garlic clove, minced
- 1 1/2 teaspoons dried thyme
- 1 teaspoon salt
- 1/4 tsp pepper

Directions:

1. Add the sliced onion to the bottom of the slow cooker. Season the chicken lightly with salt pepper and add on top of the onions.
2. In a small bowl, mix together the sauce ingredients. Pour the sauce on top

of the chicken in the slow cooker. Top with lemon slices.
3. Cook on HIGH 3-4 or on LOW 6-8hours.
4. Add artichokes. Cook an additional 30 minutes.

Nutritional Value (Amount per Serving):

Calories: 1097; Fat: 64.63; Carb: 56.35; Protein: 80.13

Crock Pot Chicken Fajitas

Prep Time: 15 Mins   Cook Time: 4 Hours   Serves: 4

Ingredients:

- 1.5 lbs boneless, skinless chicken breasts
- 1 onion, thinly sliced
- 1 red bell pepper, thinly sliced
- 1 green bell pepper, thinly sliced
- 1 can (14 oz) diced tomatoes with green chilies
- 1 packet (1.25 oz) fajita seasoning mix
- 2 tablespoons lime juice
- Flour tortillas for serving
- Sour cream, salsa, and shredded cheese for topping (optional)

Directions:

1. Place chicken breasts in the bottom of the crock pot.
2. Add sliced onion, red bell pepper, and green bell pepper on top of the chicken.
3. Sprinkle the fajita seasoning mix over the ingredients.
4. Pour diced tomatoes with green chilies and lime juice over the top.
5. Cover and cook on low for 4 hours.
6. Shred the chicken using two forks.
7. Serve the chicken and vegetable mixture in flour tortillas.
8. Top with sour cream, salsa, and shredded cheese if desired.

Nutritional Value (Amount per Serving):

Calories: 549; Fat: 18.74; Carb: 64.92; Protein: 23.58

Chapter 4: Beef, Pork, and Lamb

Cuban Ropa Vieja

Prep Time: 15 Mins   Cook Time: 4 Hours   Serves: 6

Ingredients:

- 1 tablespoon vegetable oil
- 2 pounds beef flank steak
- 1 cup beef broth
- 1 (8 ounce) can tomato sauce
- 1 (6 ounce) can tomato paste
- 1 green bell pepper, seeded and sliced into strips
- 1 small onion, sliced
- 2 cloves garlic, chopped
- 1 teaspoon ground cumin
- 1 teaspoon chopped fresh cilantro
- 1 tablespoon olive oil
- 1 tablespoon white vinegar

Directions:

1. Heat vegetable oil in a large skillet over medium-high heat. Add flank steak and cook until browned, about 4 minutes per side.
2. Transfer steak to a slow cooker; pour in beef broth and tomato sauce. Add tomato paste, bell pepper, onion, garlic, cumin, cilantro, olive oil, and vinegar; stir until well blended.
3. Cover and cook on Low for up to 10 hours, or on High for 4 hours.
4. Shred steak in the slow cooker with two forks.

Nutritional Value (Amount per Serving):

Calories: 411; Fat: 12.73; Carb: 31.91; Protein: 42.02

Beef and Rice Casserole

Prep Time: 15 Mins   Cook Time: 6-7 Hours   Serves: 6

Ingredients:

- 2 pounds beef stew meat, cubed
- 1 onion, chopped
- 2 cups long-grain white rice
- 4 cups beef broth
- 1 can (14 ounces) diced tomatoes
- 1 can (14 ounces) corn kernels, drained
- 1 teaspoon chili powder
- 1 teaspoon cumin
- 1/2 teaspoon paprika
- Salt and black pepper to taste
- Chopped fresh cilantro for garnish (optional)

Directions:

1. Place beef stew meat, chopped onion, and white rice in the crock pot.

2. Add beef broth, diced tomatoes, drained corn kernels, chili powder, cumin, paprika, salt, and black pepper.
3. Stir to combine all ingredients.
4. Cover and cook on low for 6-7 hours or until beef is tender, and rice is cooked.
5. Serve hot, garnished with chopped fresh cilantro if desired.

Nutritional Value (Amount per Serving):

Calories: 518; Fat: 17.11; Carb: 76.58; Protein: 14.42

Slow Cooker Salisbury Steak

Prep Time: 15 Mins   Cook Time: 4 Hours   Serves: 8

Ingredients:

- 2 pounds lean ground beef
- ½ cup Italian seasoned bread crumbs
- ¼ cup milk
- 1 (1 ounce) envelope dry onion soup mix
- ¼ cup all-purpose flour
- 2 tablespoons vegetable oil
- 2 (10.5 ounce) cans condensed cream of chicken soup
- ¾ cup water
- 1 (1 ounce) packet dry au jus mix

Directions:

1. Combine ground beef, bread crumbs, milk, and onion soup mix together in a large bowl until well combined; shape into 8 patties.
2. Heat oil in a large skillet over medium-high heat. Dredge patties in flour just to coat, and quickly brown on both sides in the hot skillet.
3. Place browned patties into the slow cooker, stacking alternately like a pyramid.
4. Mix condensed soup, water, and au jus mix together in a medium bowl; pour over the beef patties.
5. Cook on Low until ground beef is well done, about 4 to 5 hours.

Nutritional Value (Amount per Serving):

Calories: 428; Fat: 22.56; Carb: 19.41; Protein: 34.86

Slow-Cooker Beef and Bean Burritos

Prep Time: 20 Mins   Cook Time: 6-7 Hours   Serves: 6

Ingredients:

- 2 pounds beef stew meat, cubed
- 1 onion, chopped
- 1 can (14 ounces) diced tomatoes
- 1 can (14 ounces) pinto beans, drained and rinsed
- 1 can (4 ounces) diced green chilies
- 1 tablespoon chili powder
- 1 teaspoon cumin
- 1/2 teaspoon garlic powder
- Salt and black pepper to taste
- Flour tortillas for serving
- Shredded lettuce, diced tomatoes, shredded cheese, and sour cream for toppings

Directions:

1. Place beef stew meat, chopped onion, diced tomatoes, pinto beans, diced green chilies, chili powder, cumin, garlic powder, salt, and black pepper in the crock pot.
2. Stir to combine all ingredients.
3. Cover and cook on low for 6-7 hours or until beef is tender.
4. Serve the beef and bean mixture in flour tortillas and top with shredded lettuce, diced tomatoes, shredded cheese, and sour cream.

Nutritional Value (Amount per Serving):

Calories: 227; Fat: 14.03; Carb: 21.38; Protein: 5.47

Crock Pot Beef and Pumpkin Stew

Prep Time: 5 Mins   Cook Time: 8 Hours   Serves: 8

Ingredients:

- 2 pounds beef stew meat
- ½ teaspoon smoked paprika
- ½ teaspoon salt
- ¼ teaspoon pepper
- 3 cups radishes
- 4 cups pumpkin cubed
- 8 oz mushrooms
- 2 tablespoon tomato paste
- ¼ cup red wine vinegar
- ¼ tsp dried thyme
- 2 tablespoon garlic minced
- 4 cups beef broth
- ½ cup onion
- parsley
- 1 bay leaf

Directions:

1. Prep pumpkin and radishes by washing. Peel and cube the pumpkin, trim and cut the radishes into pieces about the same size as the pumpkin.

2. Season 2 pounds of stew beef with ½ teaspoon smoked paprika, salt and pepper to taste. Sear the seasoned beef in a skillet for 2-5 minutes until slightly browned on all sides.
3. Add to the bottom of your crock pot liner. Pan drippings and all!
4. Add 2-4 cups cleaned and trimmed radishes and 4 cups cubed pumpkin to the beef in the crock pot. Add in 8 oz mushrooms, ½ cup onion and mix to combine.
5. Add 2 tablespoons tomato paste, ¼ cup red wine vinegar, ¼ teaspoon dried thyme and 2 tablespoons minced garlic and mix well to season.
6. Pour in 4 cups beef broth and add the bay leaf. Cover and cook on low for 8 hours or on high for 4-5 hours until beef is tender.
7. Garnish with parsley, more thyme, salt and pepper if need be. Enjoy!

Nutritional Value (Amount per Serving):

Calories: 582; Fat: 39.02; Carb: 46.48; Protein: 22.35

Slow Cooker Cranberry Pork Roast

Prep Time: 15 Mins   Cook Time: 6 Hours 10 Mins   Serves: 6

Ingredients:

- 1 (16 ounce) can jellied cranberry sauce
- ½ cup cranberry juice
- ¼ cup white sugar
- 1 teaspoon dry mustard
- ¼ teaspoon ground cloves
- salt to taste
- 1 (1 1/2-pound) boneless pork loin roast
- ¼ cup water, or as needed (Optional)
- 2 tablespoons cold water
- 2 tablespoons cornstarch

Directions:

1. Mash cranberry sauce in a bowl; stir in cranberry juice, sugar, mustard, cloves, and salt.
2. Place pork roast into a slow cooker and pour cranberry mixture over top. Cook on Low for 6 to 8 hours. Transfer roast to a plate; cover and keep warm.
3. Skim fat from cranberry sauce in the slow cooker. Transfer sauce to a 2-cup liquid measure; add water if needed to reach the 2-cup mark. Pour into a saucepan and bring to a boil.
4. Whisk 2 tablespoons cold water and cornstarch into a paste; add to cranberry sauce. Cook and stir over medium-low heat until thickened, 5 to

10 minutes.

5. Slice pork and serve with cranberry sauce.

Nutritional Value (Amount per Serving):

Calories: 545; Fat: 16.98; Carb: 10.08; Protein: 83.14

Apple Butter Pork Chops

Prep Time: 10 Mins   Cook Time: 4 Hours   Serves: 6

Ingredients:

- 2 lbs. bone-in pork chops
- 1/2 tsp. salt
- 1/4 tsp. pepper
- 1 1/2 cup apple butter
- 1 yellow onion sliced
- 2 Granny Smith apples peeled and sliced
- 2 Tbsp. apple cider vinegar

Directions:

1. Add the pork chops to the slow cooker. Sprinkle over the salt and pepper.
2. Spread the apple butter over the pork chops.
3. Add the onion and apples over the pork chops, and add the apple cider vinegar over everything.
4. Cover and cook on HIGH for 4 hours or on low for 7 hours without opening the lid during the cooking time.
5. Serve and enjoy!

Nutritional Value (Amount per Serving):

Calories: 493; Fat: 18.62; Carb: 39.42; Protein: 39.42

BBQ Pork Ribs

Prep Time: 15 Mins   Cook Time: 6-8 Hours   Serves: 6

Ingredients:

- 4 pounds pork baby back ribs
- 1 onion, chopped
- 2 cloves garlic, minced
- 1 cup BBQ sauce
- 1/4 cup apple cider vinegar
- 1/4 cup brown sugar
- 1 tablespoon Worcestershire sauce
- 1 teaspoon paprika
- 1/2 teaspoon salt
- 1/2 teaspoon black pepper

Directions:

1. Cut the racks of ribs into individual sections.

2. Place the rib sections, chopped onion, and minced garlic in the crock pot.
3. In a bowl, combine BBQ sauce, apple cider vinegar, brown sugar, Worcestershire sauce, paprika, salt, and black pepper.
4. Pour the sauce mixture over the ribs.
5. Cover and cook on low for 6-8 hours or until the ribs are tender and meat falls off the bone.
6. Serve hot.

Nutritional Value (Amount per Serving):

Calories: 1100; Fat: 71.6; Carb: 24.96; Protein: 90.96

Pork Chili

Prep Time: 15 Mins   Cook Time: 6 Hours   Serves: 12

Ingredients:

- 2-1/2 pounds boneless pork, cut into 1-inch cubes
- 2 tablespoons vegetable oil
- 1 can (28 ounce) diced tomatoes, undrained
- 1 can (16 ounces) chili beans, undrained
- 1 can (8 ounces) tomato sauce
- 1/4 cup salsa
- 1/4 cup chopped onion
- 1/4 cup chopped green pepper
- 1 tablespoon chili powder
- 1 teaspoon minced jalapeno pepper
- 1/4 teaspoon garlic powder
- 1/4 teaspoon cayenne powder
- 1/4 teaspoon pepper
- 1/4 teaspoon salt

Directions:

1. In a large skillet over medium-high heat, brown pork in oil; drain. Place in a slow cooker; add remaining ingredients. Cover and cook on high for 2 hours. Reduce heat to low and cook 4 hours longer.

Nutritional Value (Amount per Serving):

Calories: 112; Fat: 4.56; Carb: 5.64; Protein: 12.06

Slow-Cooker Apricot-Glazed Pork Roast and Stuffing

Prep Time: 10 Mins   Cook Time: 7 Hours   Serves: 6

Ingredients:

- 4 cups herb-seasoned stuffing cubes
- 3/4 cup chicken broth (from 32-oz carton)
- 1/2 cup dried apricots, chopped
- 1/3 cup frozen chopped onions (from 14-oz bag)
- 1 boneless pork loin roast (2 to 2 1/2 lb), trimmed of fat
- 1/3 cup apricot jam
- 1 tablespoon balsamic vinegar

Directions:

1. Spray slow cooker with cooking spray. In cooker, mix stuffing, broth, apricots and onions. Place pork on stuffing mixture. In small bowl, mix jam and vinegar; brush over pork.
2. Cover and cook on Low heat setting 7 to 8 hours.
3. Remove pork from cooker; place on cutting board. Stir stuffing before serving. Cut pork into slices; serve with stuffing.

Nutritional Value (Amount per Serving):

Calories: 898; Fat: 17.03; Carb: 72.48; Protein: 93.08

Slow-Cooker Pineapple-Pork Tacos

Prep Time: 20 Mins   Cook Time: 7 Hours   Serves: 6

Ingredients:

- 1 lb boneless pork shoulder roast, trimmed
- 1 package (1 oz) taco seasoning mix
- 1 can (8 oz) pineapple tidbits in juice, drained
- 2 teaspoons lime juice
- 1 box (4.6 oz) Crunchy Taco Shells (12 Count)
- 3/4 cup shredded Cheddar cheese (3 oz)
- 1 1/2 cups shredded lettuce
- 3/4 cup chopped tomato
- 1/3 cup sour cream
- 1/3 cup salsa

Directions:

1. Spray a slow cooker with cooking spray. Place pork in slow cooker; sprinkle with taco seasoning mix. Cover; cook on Low heat setting 7 to 9 hours or until pork pulls apart easily with fork.
2. Remove pork from slow cooker; shred pork. Stir into liquid in slow cooker. Stir in pineapple and lime juice.
3. To serve, divide pork among taco shells (about 1/4 cup each), and top with

remaining ingredients.

Calories: 171; Fat: 5.25; Carb: 12.07; Protein: 18.68

Slow Cooker Apple Cider Pork

Prep Time: 20 Mins   Cook Time: 8 Hours   Serves: 12

Ingredients:

- 1-2 tbsp light brown sugar
- 1 tbsp kosher salt
- 2 tsp ground pepper
- 1 tsp smoked paprika
- 1 tsp ground mustard
- ½ tsp cinnamon
- 4 lb boneless Boston butt, or pork shoulder
- 1 large sweet onion, thinly sliced
- 4 cloves garlic, minced
- 2 sprigs fresh thyme, bundles with twine
- 2 c unsweetened apple cider
- 2 tbsp apple cider vinegar

Directions:

1. Mix the brown sugar, salt, pepper, paprika, mustard, and cinnamon in a small bowl until well combined.
2. Using pieces of kitchen twine, truss the pork along its length, leaving about 2" between each section. Spread the rub over the pork evenly, coating all sides.
3. Spread the onions and garlic over the bottom of the slow cooker, then nestle the pork on top with the fat cap facing up. Pour the cider and vinegar into the slow cooker, then place the thyme on top.
4. Cover and cook on low for 8 hours, or until the pork easily pulls using the tines of a fork.
5. Remove the pork from the slow cooker using tongs, then place on a cutting board. Use two forks to gently shred into large chunks. Transfer the shredded pork back to the slow cooker and toss with the onions and sauce.
6. Serve on buns with apple cider vinegar coleslaw. Enjoy!

Nutritional Value (Amount per Serving):

Calories: 465; Fat: 28.91; Carb: 9.63; Protein: 39.7

Hoisin Pork Wraps

Prep Time: 25 Mins   Cook Time: 7 Hours   Serves: 15

Ingredients:

- 1 boneless pork loin roast (3 pounds)
- 1 cup hoisin sauce, divided
- 1 tablespoon minced fresh gingerroot
- 6 cups shredded red cabbage
- 1-1/2 cups shredded carrots
- 1/4 cup thinly sliced green onions
- 3 tablespoons rice vinegar
- 4-1/2 teaspoons sugar
- 15 flour tortillas (8 inches), warmed

Directions:

1. Cut roast in half. Combine 1/3 cup hoisin sauce and ginger; rub over pork. Transfer to a slow cooker. Cover and cook on low for 7-8 hours or until pork is tender.
2. Meanwhile, in a large bowl, combine the cabbage, carrots, onions, vinegar and sugar. Chill until serving.
3. Shred meat with 2 forks and return to the slow cooker; heat through. Place 2 teaspoons remaining hoisin sauce down the center of each tortilla; top with 1/3 cup shredded pork and 1/3 cup coleslaw. Roll up.

Nutritional Value (Amount per Serving):

Calories: 390; Fat: 9.89; Carb: 35.15; Protein: 38

Chapter 5: Fish and Seafood

Crock-Pot Jambalaya Creole

Prep Time: 10 Mins   Cook Time: 4 Hours   Serves: 8

Ingredients:

- 1 small onion chopped
- 1 medium green bell pepper chopped
- 1 cup celery chopped
- 1 (28-ounce) can diced tomatoes
- 1 (12-ounce) package smoked sausage, sliced
- 1 tablespoon Creole seasoning
- 1 tablespoon parsley
- ½ teaspoon dried thyme
- 1 pound raw peeled and deveined medium shrimp, thawed if frozen
- Salt and pepper to taste
- Optional: red pepper sauce for more heat

Directions:

1. Spray slow cooker with nonstick spray. Add onion, bell pepper, celery, diced tomatoes, smoked sausage, creole seasoning, parsley, and thyme to slow cooker. Give it a quick stir.
2. Cover and cook on low setting 3 to 4 hours until vegetables are tender.
3. Add thawed shrimp to slow cooker and cook an additional 30 minutes or until shrimp are pink. Season with salt and pepper to taste. Add a few drops of red pepper hot sauce if you want more spicy heat. Enjoy!

Nutritional Value (Amount per Serving):

Calories: 69; Fat: 1.34; Carb: 5.14; Protein: 9.14

CrockPot Jambalaya Creole

Prep Time: 10 Mins   Cook Time: 4 Hours   Serves: 8

Ingredients:

- 1 small onion chopped
- 1 medium green bell pepper chopped
- 1 cup celery chopped
- 1 (28-ounce) can diced tomatoes
- 1 (12-ounce) package smoked sausage , sliced
- 1 tablespoon Creole seasoning
- 1 tablespoon parsley
- ½ teaspoon dried thyme
- 1 pound raw peeled and deveined medium shrimp thawed if frozen

- Salt and pepper to taste
- Optional: red pepper sauce for more heat!

1. Spray slow cooker with nonstick spray. Add onion, bell pepper, celery, diced tomatoes, smoked sausage, creole seasoning, parsley, and thyme to slow cooker. Give it a quick stir.
2. Cover and cook on low setting 3 to 4 hours until vegetables are tender.
3. Add thawed shrimp to slow cooker and cook an additional 30 minutes or until shrimp are pink. Season with salt and pepper to taste. Add a few drops of red pepper hot sauce if you want more spicy heat. Enjoy!

Nutritional Value (Amount per Serving):

Calories: 101; Fat: 2.8; Carb: 16.67; Protein: 3.02

Lemon and Garlic Butter Sea Scallops

Prep Time: 10 Mins   Cook Time: 45 Mins   Serves: 2

Ingredients:

- 60 grams butter, melted
- 3 cloves minced garlic
- 30ml fresh squeezed lemon juice
- 1tsp dried parsley
- 300g fresh sea scallops

Directions:

1. Combine all ingredients except scallops in mixing bowl.
2. Add scallops to slow cooker
3. Pour over the butter sauce
4. Cook on high with tea towel trick in place for 40-45 minutes approx. or until scallops are cooked through.

Nutritional Value (Amount per Serving):

Calories: 547; Fat: 27.35; Carb: 59.34; Protein: 33.89

Crock Pot New Orleans Spicy Barbecue Shrimp

Prep Time: 15 Mins   Cook Time: 30 Mins   Serves: 4

Ingredients:

- 2 cloves garlic, minced
- 1 teaspoon Cajun seasoning
- ½ cup Unsalted Butter cut into pieces
- ¼ cup Worcestershire Sauce
- 1 tablespoon hot pepper sauce
- 1 lemon juice
- Salt and pepper to taste
- 1 ½ pounds large shrimp unpeeled
- 1 green onion finely chopped

Directions:

1. Combine garlic, cajun seasoning, butter, Worcestershire Sauce, hot pepper sauce and lemon juice in the crock pot. Salt and pepper to taste. Cover and cook on high for 30 minutes or until hot.
2. Rinse shrimp and drain.
3. Spoon ½ of the sauce from the crock pot into a measuring cup.
4. Place shrimp in the crock pot and drizzle with remaining sauce.
5. Stir to coat evenly.
6. Cover and cook on high for 30 minutes until shrimp are opaque.
7. Turn to warm for serving.
8. Sprinkle with green onion before serving.

Nutritional Value (Amount per Serving):

Calories: 391; Fat: 27.35; Carb: 12.61; Protein: 24.2

Slow Cooker Red Curry with Cod

Prep Time: 15 Mins   Cook Time: 2 Hours   Serves: 4

Ingredients:

- 2 15 oz. cans light coconut milk
- 3 tbsp red curry paste
- 1 tbsp curry powder
- 1 tsp ground ginger
- 1 tsp garlic powder
- 1 red bell pepper, sliced
- 12 oz bag julienned carrots or matchstick carrots
- 1 lb. cod fish fillet
- Salt and pepper to taste
- Fresh basil and/or green onion, garnish
- 1 cup brown rice, as side dish

Directions:

1. To the slow cooker insert, add the cans of coconut milk and whisk in the curry paste, curry powder, ground ginger and garlic powder.
2. Carefully stir in the sliced bell peppers, carrots and then gently place the cod fillet into the sauce. You can add it whole, as it will be easier to break into bite size pieces after it slow cooks.
3. Set on low and cook for 2 hours. Once cooked, gently break apart the cod into bite size pieces. Season with salt and pepper to taste.
4. Prepare rice as directed on package.
5. Serve Slow Cooker Curried Cod over rice with cilantro and green onion garnish.

Calories: 774; Fat: 62.66; Carb: 33.38; Protein: 28.84

Slow Cooker Tuna Salpicao

Prep Time: 10 Mins   Cook Time: 4 Hours   Serves: 2

Ingredients:

- 250 grams tuna loin, cut into inch cubes
- 1 cup olive oil
- 1 bulb garlic, finely chopped
- 4 pieces Jalapeno peppers, finely chopped
- 3-5 pieces red chili, finely chopped
- 2 teaspoons black peppercorns, coarsely ground
- 1 teaspoon salt

Directions:

1. Combine olive oil, garlic, jalapenos, red chili, black peppercorns, and salt in the slow cooker.
2. Cook for 4 hours on low.
3. Switch heat to high.
4. Add tuna and cook for 10 minutes.

Nutritional Value (Amount per Serving):

Calories: 498; Fat: 28.76; Carb: 16.96; Protein: 45.88

Slow Cooker Salmon Curry

Prep Time: 10 Mins   Cook Time: 2 Hours 45 Mins   Serves: 6

Ingredients:

- 6 pieces salmon, without skin
- 1 onion chopped
- 6 cloves garlic chopped
- 2 teaspoons freshly grated ginger
- 3 stalks celery chopped
- 2 carrots chopped
- 2 cans coconut milk
- ½ cup vegetable stock
- 1 12 ounce can tomato paste
- 1 ½ teaspoons coriander
- 1 ½ teaspoons cumin

- 1 teaspoon chili powder, can reduce to ½ for a milder curry or eliminate entirely
- 2 teaspoons smoked paprika
- 1 teaspoon turmeric
- ½ teaspoon pepper
- ¼ teaspoon salt
- Chopped cilantro, parsley, and chili flakes to garnish

Directions:

1. Turn on slow cooker.
2. Pour in the 2 cans of coconut milk.
3. Dollop the tomato paste in.
4. Add in Vegetable stock, coriander, cumin, chili, turmeric and paprika
5. Add in salt and pepper.
6. Stir the ingredients together well.
7. Place salmon pieces into the slow cooker - trying your best for them not to overlap.
8. Add in the onions, garlic, ginger, celery and carrots.
9. Put the lid on and set the timer for 2.75 hours on low.
10. Garnish and serve with rice or naan.

Nutritional Value (Amount per Serving):

Calories: 643; Fat: 34.54; Carb: 19.37; Protein: 68.82

Crock Pot Coconut Curry Mussels

Prep Time: 15 Mins   Cook Time: 2 Hours   Serves: 4

Ingredients:

- 2 pounds mussels, cleaned and debearded
- 1 can (14 ounces) coconut milk
- 2 tablespoons red curry paste
- 1 cup diced tomatoes
- 1 cup diced onions
- 2 cloves garlic, minced
- 1 tablespoon fish sauce
- 1 tablespoon brown sugar
- 1 lime, juiced
- Fresh cilantro leaves for garnish
- Cooked rice or crusty bread for serving

Directions:

1. In your crock pot, combine the cleaned mussels, coconut milk, red curry paste, diced tomatoes, diced onions, minced garlic, fish sauce, and brown sugar.

2. Stir to combine.
3. Cover and cook on LOW for 2 hours, or until the mussels have opened and are cooked.
4. Stir in the lime juice.
5. Serve hot, garnished with fresh cilantro leaves, and provide cooked rice or crusty bread for soaking up the coconut curry sauce.

Nutritional Value (Amount per Serving):

Calories: 547; Fat: 26.74; Carb: 27.36; Protein: 50.04

Coconut Curry Crock Pot Mussels

Prep Time: 15 Mins   Cook Time: 2 Hours   Serves: 4

Ingredients:

- 2 pounds mussels, cleaned and debearded
- 1 can (14 ounces) coconut milk
- 1/2 cup diced tomatoes
- 1/2 cup diced onions
- 2 cloves garlic, minced
- 2 tablespoons red curry paste
- 1 tablespoon fish sauce
- 1 tablespoon brown sugar
- 1 lime, juiced
- Fresh cilantro leaves for garnish

Directions:

1. In your crock pot, combine the cleaned mussels, coconut milk, diced tomatoes, diced onions, minced garlic, red curry paste, fish sauce, and brown sugar.
2. Stir to combine.
3. Cover and cook on LOW for 2 hours, or until the mussels have opened and are cooked.
4. Stir in the lime juice.
5. Serve hot, garnished with fresh cilantro leaves.

Nutritional Value (Amount per Serving):

Calories: 362; Fat: 19.9; Carb: 17.86; Protein: 29.52

Crock-Pot Hot Shrimp Dip

Prep Time: 15 Mins   Cook Time: 1 Hour   Serves: 10

Ingredients:

- 1 pound pre-cooked salad shrimp (chopped (if frozen thawed))
- 8 ounces cream cheese (softened and cubed)
- 1 cup shredded Parmesan cheese

- 1 small yellow onion (peeled and diced)
- ⅓ teaspoon garlic powder

Directions:

1. Add all ingredients to a slow cooker.
2. Cover and cook on LOW for 1 hour or until all cheese is melted. Stirring occasionally.
3. Turn slow cooker to WARM setting to keep dip warm while serving for up to 2 hours.
4. Serve with sliced bread or crackers and enjoy!

Nutritional Value (Amount per Serving):

Calories: 304; Fat: 27.25; Carb: 2.95; Protein: 11.58

Slow Cooker Mussel and Potato Rice

Prep Time: 15 Mins   Cook Time: 1 Hour   Serves: 8

Ingredients:

- 1 kilogram mussels
- 1 kilogram potatoes, peeled and cut into 1/4″ discs
- 2 cups white rice
- 2 pieces shallots, finely chopped
- 1 cup white wine
- Salt to taste

Directions:

1. Line the bottom of a large rondo with chopped shallots.
2. Add the mussels and white wine. Bring to a boil then cover. Allow to steam for 5 minutes or until mussels open.
3. De-shell the mussels leaving some intact.
4. Coat your slow cooker with non-stick cooking spray.
5. Assemble the layers – potatoes, then rice, then mussels. Top with a layer of the mussels with shells on.
6. Pour in the mussel stock.
7. Cook for 1.5 hours on high.

Nutritional Value (Amount per Serving):

Calories: 378; Fat: 3.17; Carb: 64.97; Protein: 20.76

Crock Pot Low County Shrimp and Grits

Prep Time: 15 Mins   Cook Time: 10 Hours   Serves: 4-6

Ingredients:

- 6 ups chicken broth
- 3/4 teaspoon salt
- 1 1/2 ups quick-cooking grits, uncooked
- 1 green pepper, chopped
- 1/2 up red pepper, chopped
- 6 green onions, chopped
- 2 garlic cloves, minced
- 1 1/2 tbs small shrimp, peeled cleaned, vein removed
- 2 tablespoons butter
- 1 1/2 ups shredded sharp cheddar cheese (3 ounces)
- 1 1/2 ups shredded monterey jack cheese (3 ounces)
- 2 10 ounce) cans diced tomatoes and green chilies, drained
- 1/4 teaspoon cayenne pepper (optional)

Directions:

1. Combine chicken broth, salt and grits in the crock pot. Cover and cook on LOW 6-8 hours.
2. Two hours before serving, saute the peppers, onions, garlic, and shrimp in the 2 tablespoons butter until tender. Add this mixture to the crock pot along with the cheeses, tomatoes with chilies, and cayenne, if using.
3. Continue to cook on HIGH an additional 2 hours.

Nutritional Value (Amount per Serving):

Calories: 270; Fat: 13.25; Carb: 31.08; Protein: 11.48

Crock-Pot Lobster Bisque

Prep Time: 45 Mins   Cook Time: 3 Hours   Serves: 8

Ingredients:

- 2 medium shallots (finely minced)
- 1 clove garlic (finely minced)
- 29 ounces canned petite diced tomatoes (Undrained)
- 32 ounce low-sodium chicken broth
- 1 tablespoon old bay seasoning
- 1 teaspoon dried dill
- 1/4 cup chopped fresh parsley
- 1 teaspoon freshly ground black pepper
- 1/2 teaspoon ground paprika
- 4 medium lobster tails
- 1 pint heavy whipping cream

Directions:

1. Put minced shallots and garlic in a microwave safe bowl and microwave on high for 2-3 minutes or until the shallots are wilted and starting to turn translucent.
2. Add shallot and garlic mixture to a 6-quart or larger slow cooker.

3. Continue adding tomatoes, chicken broth, old bay seasoning, dill, parsley, pepper paprika to the slow cooker.
4. With a sharp knife, cut off the fan part of the very end of the lobsters, and add those to the slow cooker.
5. Stir, cover and cook on LOW for 6 hours or on HIGH for 3 hours.
6. Remove the lobster tail ends and discard.
7. Using a blender or immersion blender, puree the soup mixture to your desired chunkiness.
8. Add the soup back into the crock-pot if you used a regular blender.
9. Add your lobster tails to the soup, cover and cook 45 minutes on LOW or until the shells turn red and the lobster meat is cooked.
10. Remove lobster tails from the soup, and let cool slightly.
11. While the lobster is cooling, add the cream and stir.
12. With a sharp knife, cut each lobster tail in half long-ways, and remove the lobster flesh from the shells.
13. Discard shells and roughly chop lobster meat and add back into the soup.
14. Serve and enjoy!

Nutritional Value (Amount per Serving):

Calories: 265; Fat: 15.27; Carb: 6.4; Protein: 26.05

Crock Pot Shrimp and Mushroom Risotto

Prep Time: 15 Mins   Cook Time: 2 Hours 30 Mins   Serves: 4

Ingredients:

- 1 pound large shrimp, peeled and deveined
- 2 cups Arborio rice
- 1 cup sliced mushrooms
- 1 cup diced onions
- 2 cloves garlic, minced
- 4 cups chicken broth
- 1/2 cup dry white wine
- 1/2 cup grated Parmesan cheese
- 2 tablespoons butter
- Salt and pepper to taste
- Chopped fresh parsley for garnish

Directions:

1. In your crock pot, combine the shrimp, Arborio rice, sliced mushrooms, diced onions, minced garlic, chicken broth, dry white wine, grated Parmesan cheese, butter, salt, and pepper.
2. Stir to combine.
3. Cover and cook on LOW for 2.5 hours, or until the rice is tender and the shrimp are cooked through.
4. Serve hot, garnished with chopped fresh parsley.

Nutritional Value (Amount per Serving):

Calories: 746; Fat: 41.46; Carb: 40.85; Protein: 68.12

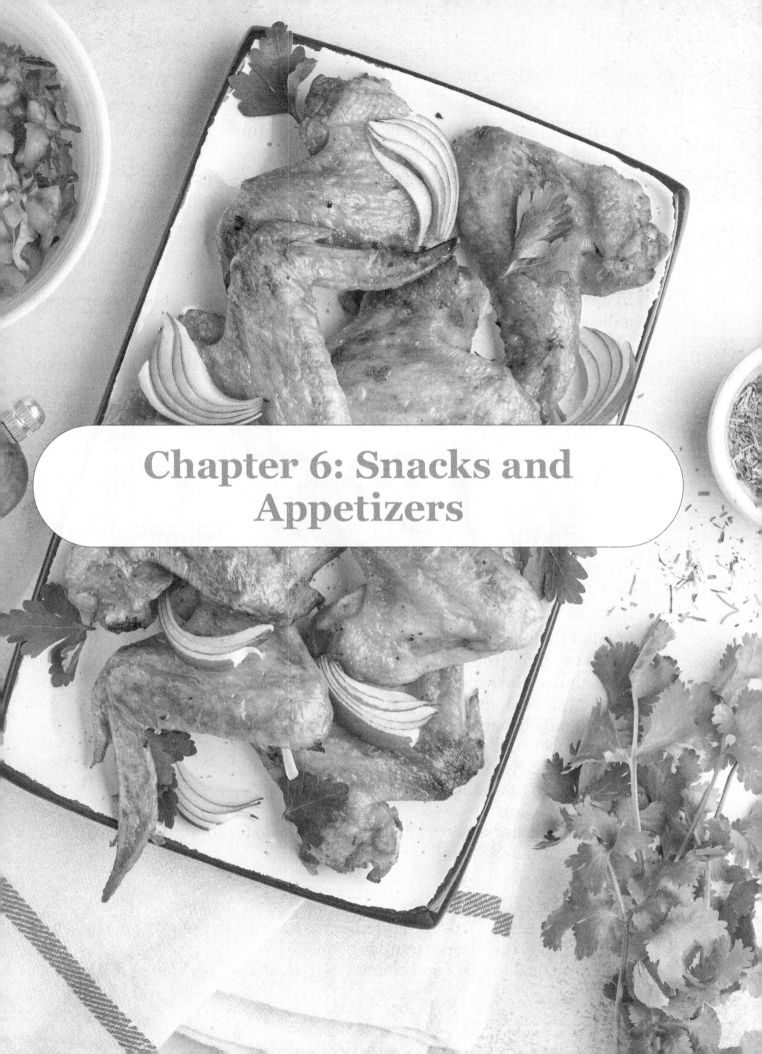

Chapter 6: Snacks and Appetizers

CrockPot Mango Salsa Chicken Wings

Prep Time: 15 Mins   Cook Time: 2 Hours 30 Mins   Serves: 6-8

Ingredients:

- 2 lbs chicken wings
- 1 cup mango salsa
- 1/4 cup honey
- 2 tablespoons soy sauce
- 2 cloves garlic, minced
- 1 teaspoon chili powder
- Chopped fresh cilantro, for garnish

Directions:

1. In a crockpot, combine the chicken wings, mango salsa, honey, soy sauce, minced garlic, and chili powder.
2. Stir to coat the chicken wings with the sauce.
3. Cook on low for 2.5 hours, stirring occasionally, until the wings are cooked through and glazed.
4. Serve the Mango Salsa Chicken Wings garnished with chopped fresh cilantro.

Nutritional Value (Amount per Serving):

Calories: 230; Fat: 5.57; Carb: 15.2; Protein: 29.18

Crockpot Sausage and Peppers Sliders

Prep Time: 10 Mins   Cook Time: 10 Hours   Serves: 6

Ingredients:

- 1 pound Italian sausage links (5 sausages)
- 2 tbsp minced garlic
- 1 (16-ounce) bag frozen pepper stir-fry (with sliced green/red/yellow peppers and onions)
- 1/2 cup mild banana pepper rings (drained)
- 1 (26-ounce) jar tomato and basil pasta sauce
- 1 (6-ounce) can tomato paste with basil, garlic and oregano
- 1 tbsp Italian seasoning (basil/oregano/thyme)
- pepper, to taste
- Provolone cheese slices or shredded mozzarella for topping (optional)
- 5 Hoagie or sandwich rolls of your choice

Directions:

1. Place sausages in slow cooker.
2. Stir in the garlic, frozen pepper mix, banana peppers, tomato sauce, tomato paste, Italian seasoning pepper
3. Cover, set heat to LOW and simmer 8-10 hours (or 4-5 hours on HIGH)

4. 20 minutes before serving, wrap your hoagie rolls in aluminum foil and throw in a 350°F oven for 10 minutes to warm (alternately, wrap two at a time in a paper towel and microwave for 20-30 seconds).
5. If desired, place a slice of provolone cheese into each hoagie roll.
6. Spoon a sausage and the red sauce pepper mixture into the hoagie rolls.
7. Top with another slice of provolone cheese or shredded mozzarella if desired.

Nutritional Value (Amount per Serving):

Calories: 339; Fat: 9.16; Carb: 44.86; Protein: 24.6

Crock Pot Grape Jelly Meatball

Prep Time: 5 Mins   Cook Time: 3 Hours 5 Mins   Serves: 8

Ingredients:

- 2 lb. frozen meatballs
- 2 c. bbq sauce
- 1 (12-oz.) jar grape jelly
- 1/4 c. sriracha

Directions:

1. Place meatballs in bowl of a slow cooker and pour BBQ sauce, grape jelly, and sriracha over. Stir to coat meatballs.
2. Cook on low for 3 to 4 hours. Stir meatballs before serving.

Nutritional Value (Amount per Serving):

Calories: 347; Fat: 25.31; Carb: 14.46; Protein: 17.34

Slow Cooker Thai Chicken Satay Skewers

Prep Time: 20 Mins   Cook Time: 3 Hours   Serves: 6-8

Ingredients:

- 2 lbs boneless, skinless chicken thighs, cut into strips
- 1 cup coconut milk
- 1/4 cup creamy peanut butter
- 2 tablespoons soy sauce
- 2 tablespoons brown sugar
- 1 tablespoon red curry paste
- Bamboo skewers, soaked in water
- Chopped peanuts and cilantro, for garnish
- Peanut sauce, for dipping

Directions:

1. In a crockpot, combine the chicken strips, coconut milk, peanut butter, soy

sauce, brown sugar, and red curry paste.
2. Stir to coat the chicken with the sauce.
3. Cook on low for 3 hours, stirring occasionally, until the chicken is cooked through and the sauce is creamy.
4. Thread the chicken strips onto soaked bamboo skewers.
5. Serve the Thai Chicken Satay Skewers garnished with chopped peanuts and cilantro, along with peanut sauce for dipping.

Nutritional Value (Amount per Serving):

Calories: 412; Fat: 23.26; Carb: 35.96; Protein: 17.38

Slow Cooker Baby Back Ribs

Prep Time: 25 Mins   Cook Time: 6 Hours   Serves: 8

Ingredients:

- 1 tbsp garlic powder
- 2 tsp smoked paprika
- 1 tsp ground mustard
- 2 tsp chili powder
- ½ tsp cayenne pepper
- 1 tbsp onion powder
- 1 tsp red pepper flakes
- Salt and pepper (to taste)

- ⅓cup brown sugar
- 2 cups BBQ Sauce
- ⅓cup apple cider vinegar
- 3 tbsp Worcestershire sauce
- ¼ cup whiskey (use beef broth for an alcohol free option)
- 1 slab baby back ribs

Directions:

1. Remove the silver skin on the back of the ribs. Pat the ribs dry and season both sides of the ribs with salt and pepper.
2. Them combine garlic powder, smoked paprika, ground mustard, chili powder, cayenne powder, onion powder, and red pepper flakes in a small bowl. Mix seasonings together and coat both sides of the ribs with the dry rub.
3. Pour your favorite BBQ sauce into the slow cooker along with brown sugar, apple cider vinegar, a splash of whiskey, and some Worcestershire sauce. Whisk everything together.
4. Cut the slab of ribs in half, and then place half of the ribs on the bottom of the slow cooker and the other half on top. Spoon the BBQ sauce on top of the ribs and then cover with the lid.
5. Cook on low for 6 hours.
6. Once ribs are finished cooking, place ribs on a baking sheet lined with aluminum foil. Coat with remaining BBQ sauce/braising liquid from the crockpot. Broil the ribs in the oven for 3-5 minutes on the middle rack.

Nutritional Value (Amount per Serving):

Calories: 518; Fat: 31.17; Carb: 21.23; Protein: 40.25

Crock-Pot Candied Spiced Nuts

Prep Time: 10 Mins   Cook Time: 3 Hours   Serves: 3

Ingredients:

- 2 cups raw almonds
- 1.5 cups raw pecans
- ¾ cup brown sugar
- ¼ cup granulated sugar
- 2 teaspoons ground cinnamon
- ¼ cup water
- ½ teaspoon ground ginger
- ½ teaspoon ground nutmeg

Directions:

1. Lightly grease the slow cooker bowl. Place nuts in the slow cooker.
2. In a small bowl, mix both sugars and cinnamon and add to slow cooker. Stir together to mix well.
3. Add water and stir well again.
4. Set the slow cooker on HIGH and cook for 3 hours. Stir every 20 to 30 minutes.
5. Once done, place nuts on a large parchment paper lined sheet. Sprinkle with nutmeg and ginger, gently toss. Let nuts cool completely.
6. Store in air tight container.

Nutritional Value (Amount per Serving):

Calories: 595; Fat: 36.19; Carb: 71.09; Protein: 4.89

Spinach and Artichoke Stuffed Mushrooms

Prep Time: 15 Mins   Cook Time: 2 Hours   Serves: 4-6

Ingredients:

- 20-24 large mushrooms, cleaned and stems removed
- 1 (10 oz) package frozen chopped spinach, thawed and drained
- 1 (14 oz) can artichoke hearts, drained and chopped
- 1 cup cream cheese, softened
- 1/2 cup grated Parmesan cheese
- 2 cloves garlic, minced
- Salt and pepper to taste

Directions:

1. In a bowl, combine the chopped spinach, chopped artichoke hearts, cream cheese, grated Parmesan cheese, minced garlic, salt, and pepper.
2. Stuff each mushroom cap with the spinach and artichoke mixture.
3. Place the stuffed mushrooms in the crockpot.
4. Cook on low for 2 hours until the mushrooms are tender and the filling is hot and bubbly.

Slow Cooker Pizza Dip

Prep Time: 15 Mins   Cook Time: 2 Hours   Serves: 6-8

Ingredients:

- 8 oz cream cheese, softened
- 1 cup ricotta cheese
- 1 cup shredded mozzarella cheese
- 1/4 cup grated Parmesan cheese
- 1 cup pizza sauce
- 1/2 cup sliced pepperoni
- 1/4 cup sliced black olives
- 1/4 cup sliced green bell peppers
- 1/4 cup sliced red onion
- Italian seasoning, for garnish
- Breadsticks or tortilla chips, for dipping

Directions:

1. In a crockpot, combine the softened cream cheese, ricotta cheese, shredded mozzarella cheese, grated Parmesan cheese, and pizza sauce.
2. Stir to mix the ingredients.
3. Top with sliced pepperoni, sliced black olives, sliced green bell peppers, and sliced red onion.
4. Cook on low for 2 hours, or until the dip is hot and bubbly.
5. Garnish with Italian seasoning before serving.
6. Serve the Pizza Dip with breadsticks or tortilla chips for dipping.

Nutritional Value (Amount per Serving):

Calories: 225; Fat: 15.48; Carb: 8.15; Protein: 13.51

Slow Cooker Sweet and Spicy Meatballs

Prep Time: 10 Mins   Cook Time: 3 Hours   Serves: 6-8

Ingredients:

- 1.5 lbs frozen meatballs
- 1 cup grape jelly
- 1/2 cup chili sauce
- 2 tablespoons sriracha sauce (adjust to taste)

Directions:

1. In a crockpot, combine the frozen meatballs, grape jelly, chili sauce, and sriracha sauce.
2. Stir to coat the meatballs with the sauce.
3. Cook on low for 3 hours, stirring occasionally, until the meatballs are

heated through and the sauce has thickened.

Nutritional Value (Amount per Serving):

Calories: 314; Fat: 21.71; Carb: 15.63; Protein: 14.69

Crock Pot Street Corn Dip

Prep Time: 15 Mins   Cook Time: 2 Hours 30 Mins   Serves: 12

Ingredients:

- 8 oz cream cheese
- 3 cups frozen corn
- 1 jalapeno de seeded diced
- 1/4 cup mayonnaise
- 1/4 cup sour cream
- 1/4 cup finely diced red onion
- 1/4 cup chopped fresh cilantro
- 2 garlic cloves minced
- 4 oz block of mild cheddar cheese
- 4 oz block of pepper jack cheese
- 1 lime juiced
- 1 tsp salt
- ½ tsp chili powder
- ⅛ tsp cayenne pepper
- Cotija cheese to top it with

Directions:

1. With a cheese grater, grate the 4 oz of cheddar cheese and jalapeno pepper cheese. You want them in block form,not pre shredded. Pre shredded won't melt as well. Then set aside.
2. In crock pot,add in cream cheese, frozen corn, jalapeno de seeded diced, sour cream, mayonnaise, finely diced red onion, garlic cloves minced, shredded cheese, juice of 1 lime, salt, chili powder cayenne pepper.
3. Place on low for 2 hours. Stirring once after 30 minutes,and then another time 30 minutes later.
4. Once the dip is done, stir in cilantro, add to a serving bowl and top with cotija cheese and enjoy!

Nutritional Value (Amount per Serving):

Calories: 203; Fat: 13.79; Carb: 12.9; Protein: 7.64

Slow Cooked Peach Salsa

Prep Time: 20 Mins   Cook Time: 3 Hours   Serves: 11

Ingredients:

- 4 pounds tomatoes (about 12 medium), chopped
- 1 medium onion, chopped
- 4 jalapeno peppers, seeded and finely chopped
- 1/2 to 2/3 cup packed brown sugar

- 1/4 cup minced fresh cilantro
- 4 garlic cloves, minced
- 1 teaspoon salt
- 4 cups chopped peeled fresh peaches (about 4 medium), divided
- 1 can (6 ounces) tomato paste

Directions:

1. In a slow cooker, combine the first 7 ingredients; stir in 2 cups peaches. Cook, covered, on low 3-4 hours or until onion is tender.
2. Stir tomato paste and remaining peaches into slow cooker. Cool. Transfer to covered containers. (If freezing, use freezer-safe containers and fill to within 1/2 in. of tops.) Refrigerate up to 1 week or freeze up to 12 months. Thaw frozen salsa in refrigerator before serving.

Nutritional Value (Amount per Serving):

Calories: 138; Fat: 0.53; Carb: 34.51; Protein: 2.78

Crock Pot Rotel Dip

Prep Time: 15 Mins   Cook Time: 2 Hours   Serves: 12

Ingredients:

- 1 pound ground beef
- 32 oz Velveeta Cheese
- 1 can Rotel 10 oz

Directions:

1. In a large Skillet brown the ground beef. Drain any fat.
2. Cube the Velveeeta cheese and place in a crock pot.
3. Place the browned grounded beef on top.
4. Pour rotel on top.
5. Place the lid on top and cook on low for 2 hours or high for 1 hour until cheese is melted (stirring occasionally).

Nutritional Value (Amount per Serving):

Calories: 264; Fat: 14.13; Carb: 8.92; Protein: 24.36

Crock Pot Chex Mix

Prep Time: 5 Mins   Cook Time: 3 Hours   Serves: 14

Ingredients:

- 9 cups Chex cereal any combination of corn, rice, and wheat
- 2 cups tiny pretzels
- 1 ½ cups cheese snack crackers

- 1 ½ cups mixed nuts
- ½ cup butter melted
- ¼ cup Worcestershire sauce
- 3 teaspoons seasoning salt
- 1 teaspoon garlic powder
- ½ teaspoon onion powder

Directions:

1. Add Chex, pretzels, crackers, and nuts to the crock of a slow cooker, stirring well.
2. In a small bowl, whisk together butter, Worcestershire sauce, seasoning salt, garlic powder, and onion powder until well combined and dissolved.
3. Drizzle the butter sauce evenly over the top of the mixture. Toss well to combine.
4. Cover and slow cook on low for 3 hours, stirring every 45 minutes so that the mixture does not burn.
5. Spread the mixture out onto two parchment-lined baking sheets to cool to room temperature.
6. Store leftover mix in a sealed container for up to 3 weeks.

Nutritional Value (Amount per Serving):

Calories: 261; Fat: 18.17; Carb: 23.12; Protein: 3.23

Slow Cooker Coconut Curry Meatballs

Prep Time: 20 Mins   Cook Time: 8 Hours   Serves: 8

Ingredients:

- 2 tbsp olive oil
- 2 medium onions, chopped
- 6 cloves garlic, peeled and crushed
- 1 tbsp curry powder
- 4 pieces plum tomatoes, diced
- 1 tbsp brown sugar
- 1 ½ tsp salt, or to taste
- 1 can coconut milk
- 2.2 lbs (1 kilo) ground beef
- 1 cup oatmeal
- 2 tsp ground nutmeg
- 1 tsp ground cinnamon
- ½ tsp ground coriander
- 1 tsp salt, or to taste
- 3 tbsp fruit chutney
- 2 large eggs, beaten
- 2 tbsp rice vinegar

Directions:

1. Heat oil in a deep/large oven proof pan. Sauté the garlic and onions until tender about 5 minutes. Add the curry powder and coat the onion and garlic and cook just until aromatic, a minute or less.
2. Add the tomatoes, sugar, and salt. Stir. Cover and simmer in the lowest setting. In the meantime prepare the meatballs.

3. Mix the rest of the ingredients (except the coconut milk) and form into meatballs. Using a large cookie scooper (for uniformity) would produce between 28-30 meatballs.
4. Place the meatballs in the slow cooker. Pour the heated tomato curry mixture on top. Cook for 6-8 hours on low or 3 hours on high until the meatballs are tender.
5. Pour in the coconut milk and cook for another 30 minutes on high or until fully heated through. Taste and adjust seasoning if needed. Serve with rice on the side.

Nutritional Value (Amount per Serving):

Calories: 500; Fat: 32.5; Carb: 17.7; Protein: 34.22

CrockPot Hawaiian BBQ Meatballs

Prep Time: 10 Mins   Cook Time: 3 Hours   Serves: 6-8

Ingredients:

- 1.5 lbs frozen meatballs
- 1 cup barbecue sauce
- 1/2 cup pineapple juice
- 1/4 cup brown sugar
- 1/4 cup soy sauce
- 1 cup pineapple chunks

Directions:

1. In a crockpot, combine the frozen meatballs, barbecue sauce, pineapple juice, brown sugar, and soy sauce.
2. Stir to coat the meatballs with the sauce.
3. Add the pineapple chunks.
4. Cook on low for 3 hours, stirring occasionally, until the meatballs are heated through and the sauce is thickened.
5. Serve the Hawaiian BBQ Meatballs with toothpicks for easy snacking.

Nutritional Value (Amount per Serving):

Calories: 445; Fat: 23.54; Carb: 45.03; Protein: 15.2

Chapter 7: Vegetables and Sides

Slow Cooker Braised Asian Kale

Prep Time: 10 Mins   Cook Time: 2 Hours 30 Mins   Serves: 4

Ingredients:

- 1 ½ cups low-sodium chicken broth
- 3 cloves garlic, minced
- 1 tablespoon soy sauce
- 1 tablespoon minced lemongrass
- ½ teaspoon ground ginger
- 6 cups tightly packed kale, stems removed
- 1 tablespoon rice vinegar, or more to taste (Optional)

Directions:

1. Combine broth, garlic, soy sauce, lemongrass, and ginger in a slow cooker. Heat on High until flavors combine, about 30 minutes.
2. Add kale and stir to coat. Reduce heat to Low and cook for approximately 2 hours.
3. Finish with a splash of rice vinegar before serving.

Nutritional Value (Amount per Serving):

Calories: 147; Fat: 3.87; Carb: 20.85; Protein: 9.52

Slow Cooker Cheesy Creamed Corn

Prep Time: 15 Mins   Cook Time: 4 Hours   Serves: 8-10

Ingredients:

- 1 (24-ounce) bag frozen corn, about 5 ½ cups
- 1 (8-ounce) package of cream cheese, cut into small cubes
- 4 tablespoons butter, diced
- ½ cup milk
- 1 teaspoon sugar
- ½ teaspoon salt
- Freshly ground black pepper
- 1 to 2 fresh jalapeños, minced (seeds membranes removed)
- 1 cup shredded sharp cheddar cheese

Directions:

1. In a medium to large slow cooker, combine corn, cream cheese, butter, milk, sugar, salt, pepper, and minced jalapenos. Cover and cook on LOW for 4 hours. Add shredded cheddar cheese; stir until cheese is completely melted and sauce is creamy. Adjust seasonings, adding more salt and/or pepper, if desired, and stir in a bit more milk if sauce is too thick. Transfer

corn to a serving dish and serve immediately, or serve directly from the slow cooker set to WARM.

Nutritional Value (Amount per Serving):

Calories: 242; Fat: 15.73; Carb: 14.18; Protein: 11.56

Crock Pot Creamy Parmesan Polenta

Prep Time: 15 Mins   Cook Time: 3 Hours   Serves: 6

Ingredients:

- 1 cup of polenta (cornmeal)
- 4 cups of chicken or vegetable broth
- 1 cup of grated Parmesan cheese
- 2 tablespoons of butter
- 1/2 cup of heavy cream
- Salt and black pepper to taste
- Chopped fresh basil leaves for garnish (optional)

Directions:

1. In the crock pot, combine the polenta (cornmeal) and chicken or vegetable broth.
2. Stir well to mix.
3. Cover and cook on low for 3 hours or until the polenta is creamy and cooked.
4. Stir in the grated Parmesan cheese, butter, heavy cream, salt, and black pepper until the polenta is creamy and well combined.
5. Garnish with chopped fresh basil leaves before serving, if desired.

Nutritional Value (Amount per Serving):

Calories: 333; Fat: 17.26; Carb: 34.15; Protein: 10.77

French Dip Sandwiches with Onions

Prep Time: 30 Mins   Cook Time: 7 Hours   Serves: 14

Ingredients:

- 2 large onions, cut into 1/4-inch slices
- 1/4 cup butter, cubed
- 1 beef rump roast or bottom round roast (3 to 4 pounds)
- 5 cups water
- 1/2 cup soy sauce
- 1 envelope onion soup mix

- 1-1/2 teaspoons browning sauce, optional
- 1 garlic clove, minced
- 14 French rolls, split
- 2 cups shredded Swiss cheese

Directions:

1. In a large skillet, saute onions in butter until tender. Transfer to a slow cooker. Cut roast in half; place over onions.
2. In a large bowl, combine the water, soy sauce, soup mix, browning sauce if desired and garlic; pour over roast. Cover and cook on low until meat are tender, 7-9 hours.
3. Remove roast with a slotted spoon and let stand for 15 minutes. Thinly slice meat across the grain. Place on roll bottoms; sprinkle with Swiss cheese. Place on an ungreased baking sheet.
4. Broil 3-4 in. from the heat until cheese is melted, about 1 minute. Replace tops. Skim fat from cooking juices; strain and serve as a dipping sauce if desired.

Nutritional Value (Amount per Serving):

Calories: 322; Fat: 14.59; Carb: 27.53; Protein: 19.43

Slow Cooker Sweet Potatoes (Yams) and Marshmallows

Prep Time: 5 Mins   Cook Time: 3 Hours 15 Mins   Serves: 8

Ingredients:

- Cooking spray
- 2 (29 ounce) cans sweet potatoes, drained
- ⅓ cup butter, cut into 1/4-inch pieces
- ¾ cup light brown sugar
- 1 (16 ounce) package miniature marshmallows

Directions:

1. Spray the inside of a slow cooker with cooking spray.
2. Place sweet potatoes in a slow cooker and arrange butter on top of sweet potatoes. Sprinkle brown sugar over sweet potatoes.
3. Cook on High, 3 to 3 1/2 hours. Add marshmallows and cook until soft and somewhat puffy, about 15 minutes.

Nutritional Value (Amount per Serving):

Calories: 208; Fat: 8.52; Carb: 30.86; Protein: 2.89

Crock Pot Creamed Corn

Prep Time: 10 Mins   Cook Time: 4 Hours   Serves: 6

Ingredients:

- 28-32 ounces frozen whole kernel corn
- 8 ounces cream cheese at room temp, cut into pieces
- 1/4 cup butter
- 1 can evaporated milk 4 ounces
- 1 tablespoon sugar
- salt and pepper to taste

Directions:

1. Place corn in the slow cooker and add other ingredients over the top.
2. Cook on high for 2-3 hours or on low for 3-6 hours, stirring from time to time. Enjoy!

Nutritional Value (Amount per Serving):

Calories: 280; Fat: 19.35; Carb: 23.41; Protein: 2.75

Slow Cooker Creamy Mushroom Risotto

Prep Time: 15 Mins   Cook Time: 2 Hours 30 Mins   Serves: 6

Ingredients:

- 2 cups of Arborio rice
- 8 ounces of cremini mushrooms, sliced
- 1 small onion, finely chopped
- 4 cups of vegetable broth
- 1 cup of dry white wine
- 1/2 cup of grated Parmesan cheese
- 2 tablespoons of olive oil
- 2 cloves of garlic, minced
- 2 tablespoons of butter
- Salt and black pepper to taste
- Chopped fresh parsley for garnish (optional)

Directions:

1. In a skillet, heat the olive oil over medium heat. Add the sliced mushrooms and cook until they release their moisture and turn golden brown. Remove from heat and set aside.
2. In the crock pot, combine the Arborio rice, chopped onion, minced garlic, vegetable broth, dry white wine, and cooked mushrooms.
3. Stir well to mix.

4. Cover and cook on low for 2.5 hours, stirring occasionally until the rice is creamy and tender.
5. Stir in the grated Parmesan cheese and butter until melted and creamy.
6. Season with salt and black pepper to taste.
7. Garnish with chopped fresh parsley before serving, if desired.

Nutritional Value (Amount per Serving):

Calories: 418; Fat: 23.28; Carb: 54.29; Protein: 15.88

Slow Cooker Coconut Quinoa Curry

Prep Time: 20 Mins   Cook Time: 4 Hours   Serves: 8

Ingredients:

- 1 medium sweet potato peeled + chopped (about 3 cups)
- 1 large broccoli crown cut into florets (about 2 cups)
- 1/2 white onion diced (about 1 cup)
- 1 15 oz can organic chickpeas, drained and rinsed
- 1 28 oz can diced tomatoes
- 2 14.5 oz cans coconut milk (either full fat or lite)
- 1/4 cup quinoa
- 2 garlic cloves minced (about 1 tablespoon)
- 1 tablespoon freshly grated ginger
- 1 tablespoon freshly grated turmeric or 1 teaspoon ground
- 2 teaspoon wheat free tamari sauce
- 1 teaspoon miso or additional tamari
- 1/2 - 1 teaspoon chili flakes

Directions:

1. Add all ingredients to a slow cooker. Stir until everything is fully incorporated.
2. Turn the slow cooker to high and cook for 3 - 4 hours until sweet potato cooks through and the curry has thickened.

Nutritional Value (Amount per Serving):

Calories: 265; Fat: 16.5; Carb: 25.84; Protein: 7.3

Frijoles a la Charra

Prep Time: 15 Mins   Cook Time: 5 Hours   Serves: 8

Ingredients:

- 1 pound dry pinto beans
- 5 cloves garlic, chopped

- 1 teaspoon salt
- ½ pound bacon, diced
- 1 onion, chopped
- 2 fresh tomatoes, diced
- 1 (3.5 ounce) can sliced jalapeno peppers
- 1 (12 fluid ounce) can beer
- ⅓cup chopped fresh cilantro

Directions:

1. Place pinto beans in a slow cooker, and completely cover with water. Mix in garlic and salt. Coverand cook 1 hour on High.
2. Cook the bacon in a skillet over medium high heat until evenly brown, but still tender. Drain about half the fat. Place onion in the skillet, and cook until tender. Mix in tomatoes and jalapenos, and cook until heated through. Transfer to the slow cooker, stirring into the beans.
3. Cover slow cooker, and continue cooking 4 hours on Low. Mix in the beer and cilantro about 30 minutes before the end of the cook time.

Nutritional Value (Amount per Serving):

Calories: 241; Fat: 13.54; Carb: 21.34; Protein: 10.7

Paddy's Reuben Dip

Prep Time: 5 Mins   Cook Time: 2 Hours   Serves: 4

Ingredients:

- 4 packages (2 ounces each) thinly sliced deli corned beef, finely chopped
- 1 package (8 ounces) cream cheese, cubed
- 1 can (8 ounces) sauerkraut, rinsed and drained
- 1 cup sour cream
- 1 cup shredded Swiss cheese
- Rye bread or crackers

Directions:

1. In a slow cooker, combine the first 5 ingredients. Cover and cook on low for 2 hours or until cheese is melted; stir until blended. Serve warm with bread or crackers.

Nutritional Value (Amount per Serving):

Calories: 420; Fat: 31.6; Carb: 13.54; Protein: 21.54

Italian Beef Hoagies

Prep Time: 25 Mins   Cook Time: 8 Hours   Serves: 18

Ingredients:

- 1 beef sirloin tip roast (4 pounds), halved

- 2 envelopes Italian salad dressing mix
- 2 cups water
- 1 jar (16 ounces) mild pickled pepper rings, undrained
- 18 hoagie buns, split

Directions:

1. Place roast in a slow cooker. Combine the salad dressing mix and water; pour over roast. Cover and cook on low for 8-10 hours or until meat is tender.
2. Remove meat; shred with 2 forks and return to the slow cooker. Add pepper rings; heat through. Spoon 1/2 cup meat mixture onto each bun.

Nutritional Value (Amount per Serving):

Calories: 93; Fat: 4.39; Carb: 3.6; Protein: 9.19

Potluck Macaroni and Cheese

Prep Time: 25 Mins   Cook Time: 2 Hours   Serves: 16

Ingredients:

- 3 cups uncooked elbow macaroni
- 1 package (16 ounces) Velveeta, cubed
- 2 cups shredded Mexican cheese blend
- 2 cups shredded white cheddar cheese
- 1-3/4 cups whole milk
- 1 can (12 ounces) evaporated milk
- 3/4 cup butter, melted
- 3 large eggs, lightly beaten

Directions:

1. Cook macaroni according to package directions for al dente; drain. Transfer to a greased slow cooker. Stir in remaining ingredients.
2. Cook, covered, on low 2 to 2-1/2 hours or until a thermometer reads at least 160°, stirring once.

Nutritional Value (Amount per Serving):

Calories: 237; Fat: 15; Carb: 17.89; Protein: 7.7

Crock Pot Herb Roasted Potatoes

Prep Time: 10 Mins   Cook Time: 5 Hours   Serves: 4-6

Ingredients:

- 6 medium potatoes
- ¼ cup water

- 1 teaspoon salt
- 1 teaspoon pepper

- 1 teaspoon garlic powder
- 1 teaspoon instant minced onion
- ½ teaspoon dried dill
- 1 teaspoon Italian seasoning
- 1 teaspoon dried parsley
- 4 tablespoons butte

Directions:

1. Chop potatoes into half moons (slice potato in half longways, then into pieces). Place into crock pot.
2. Add water and sprinkle with all the herbs and seasoning. Stir to distribute the herbs.
3. Add butter in separate pieces on top of the potatoes.
4. Cover and cook on low for 5 hours or until tender.

Nutritional Value (Amount per Serving):

Calories: 766; Fat: 26.72; Carb: 84.24; Protein: 46.96

Slow Cooker Lemon Herb Couscous

Prep Time: 10 Mins   Cook Time: 2 Hours   Serves: 84

Ingredients:

- 1 cup of couscous
- 2 cups of vegetable broth
- Zest and juice of 1 lemon
- 2 tablespoons of chopped fresh parsley
- 1 tablespoon of chopped fresh basil
- 1 tablespoon of chopped fresh thyme
- 2 tablespoons of olive oil
- Salt and black pepper to taste
- Lemon wedges for garnish (optional)

Directions:

1. In the crock pot, combine the couscous, vegetable broth, lemon zest, lemon juice, chopped fresh parsley, chopped fresh basil, chopped fresh thyme, olive oil, salt, and black pepper.
2. Stir well to mix.
3. Cover and cook on low for 2 hours or until the couscous is fluffy and infused with the herbs and lemon.
4. Serve with lemon wedges for garnish, if desired.

Nutritional Value (Amount per Serving):

Calories: 6; Fat: 0.33; Carb: 0.65; Protein: 0.09

Chapter 8: Beans and Grains

Vegan Slow Cooker Wild Rice Pilaf

Prep Time: 10 Mins   Cook Time: 6 Hours   Serves: 4

Ingredients:

- 1 cup wild rice, rinsed and drained
- 1 onion, chopped
- 3 cloves garlic, minced
- 1 cup sliced mushrooms
- 2 cups vegetable broth
- 1 tbsp olive oil
- 1 tsp thyme
- salt and pepper to taste

Directions:

1. In a slow cooker, add wild rice, onion, garlic, mushrooms, vegetable broth, olive oil, thyme, and salt and pepper.
2. Stir to combine.
3. Cover and cook on high for 4 hours or on low for 6 hours.
4. Once cooked, stir and adjust seasoning as desired.
5. Serve hot.

Nutritional Value (Amount per Serving):

Calories: 198; Fat: 3.88; Carb: 35.94; Protein: 6.62

Slow Cooker Black Bean Soup

Prep Time: 20 Mins   Cook Time: 7 Hours   Serves: 8

Ingredients:

- 1 lb. dried black beans
- 6 cups chicken broth
- 14 oz. petite diced tomatoes
- 1 large ham hock
- ½ cup white onion diced
- 2 Tbsp. jalapeno minced
- 1 garlic clove minced
- 2 tsp. chili powder
- ½ tsp. onion powder
- ¼ tsp. pepper
- ¼ cup cilantro chopped
- ¼ tsp. salt to taste
- cheddar cheese
- steamed rice
- tortillas and tortilla chips

Directions:

1. Rinse the beans and add them to the slow cooker. No need to soak. If you want to soak the beans overnight, you can, but drain the beans before starting the recipe.
2. Add the chicken broth, diced tomatoes, ham hock, onion, jalapeno, garlic, chili powder, onion powder, and pepper.
3. Cover and cook on HIGH for 7 hours without opening the lid during the cooking time.
4. Remove the ham hock onto a plate, remove any meat you can find off the

ham hock, shred and put into the beans.

5. Add the cilantro, stir
6. Taste for salt, adding the desired amount.
7. Serve and enjoy!

Nutritional Value (Amount per Serving):

Calories: 514; Fat: 14.47; Carb: 42.07; Protein: 52.88

Slow-Cooked Vegan Spanish Rice and Beans

Prep Time: 20 Mins   Cook Time: 4 Hours   Serves: 6

Ingredients:

- 2 cups long-grain rice
- 4 cups vegetable broth
- 2 cans (15 oz each) black beans, drained and rinsed
- 1 can (14 oz) diced tomatoes
- 1 onion, diced
- 2 cloves garlic, minced
- 1 teaspoon smoked paprika
- Salt and pepper to taste
- Chopped fresh cilantro for garnish

Directions:

1. In the crock pot, combine long-grain rice, vegetable broth, black beans, diced tomatoes, diced onion, minced garlic, smoked paprika, salt, and pepper.
2. Stir well, cover, and cook on low for 4 hours.
3. Garnish with chopped fresh cilantro before serving this flavorful Spanish rice and beans.

Nutritional Value (Amount per Serving):

Calories: 384; Fat: 5.17; Carb: 67.29; Protein: 17.4

Kosher Vegetarian Bean Cholent

Prep Time: 20 Mins   Cook Time: 4 Hours   Serves: 12

Ingredients:

- 1/2 cup dried red beans
- 1/2 cup dried white beans
- 1/2 cup dried garbanzo beans
- 2 tablespoons oil
- 2 large onions, diced
- 1/2 cup barley
- 4 medium potatoes, peeled and sliced

- 2 tablespoons onion soup powder
- 1 (15-ounce) can diced tomatoes

Directions:

1. Soak the beans in water overnight.
2. When ready to cook, drain the beans.
3. Heat oil in a skillet. Sauté onions for 5 to 7 minutes until translucent.
4. In a crock pot, mix onions with beans and barley. Add water to cover. Bring to a boil. Lower heat and cook, covered, for 30 minutes.
5. Add potatoes. Cook, covered, on low heat for 30 more minutes.
6. Stir in onion soup mix and tomatoes. Cook, tightly covered, on low heat for several hours or (if you plan to serve it for Sabbath lunch) overnight.

Nutritional Value (Amount per Serving):

Calories: 305; Fat: 5.85; Carb: 52.85; Protein: 12.09

Slow-Cooked Vegan Black Eyed Peas

Prep Time: 15 Mins   Cook Time: 6 Hours   Serves: 6

Ingredients:

- 1 pound bag dried black-eyed peas
- 2 cups water
- 2 cups vegetable broth.
- 1 small onion, diced
- 1 clove garlic, finely diced
- 1 bay leaf
- 1 teaspoon hot sauce such as
- Sriracha
- 1 teaspoon ground sage
- 1 teaspoon salt
- ½ teaspoon pepper
- ½ teaspoon paprika
- ⅛ teaspoon dried thyme
- ⅛ teaspoon liquid smoke

Directions:

1. Put the black-eyed peas in a large bowl and cover with water to clean. Swish your hand around in the water and pick out any beans that don't look good or that float.
2. Drain the beans. Put the beans in a very large pot or bowl. Cover with fresh water by about 4 inches above the beans.
3. Let soak on the counter overnight. They will plump up.
4. Drain the pre-soaked black eyed peas and put them in the slow cooker.
5. Add the onion, garlic and spices to the crockpot. Add 2 cups of vegetable broth. Now add enough water to just cover the beans. You may also use more broth instead.
6. Turn on low for about 6 to 8 hours.
7. Give a bean a pinch at the end of cooking to make sure they are the softness that you like.

Nutritional Value (Amount per Serving):

Calories: 49; Fat: 0.64; Carb: 8.69; Protein: 2.58

Party Time Beans

Prep Time: 10 Mins   Cook Time: 5 Hours   Serves: 16

Ingredients:

- 1-1/2 cups ketchup
- 1 medium onion, chopped
- 1 medium green pepper, chopped
- 1 medium sweet red pepper, chopped
- 1/2 cup water
- 1/2 cup packed brown sugar
- 2 bay leaves
- 2 to 3 teaspoons cider vinegar
- 1 teaspoon ground mustard
- 1/8 teaspoon pepper
- 1 can (16 ounces) kidney beans, rinsed and drained
- 1 can (15-1/2 ounces) great northern beans, rinsed and drained
- 1 can (15-1/4 ounces) lima beans
- 1 can (15 ounces) black beans, rinsed and drained
- 1 can (15-1/2 ounces) black-eyed peas, rinsed and drained

Directions:

1. In a slow cooker, combine the first 10 ingredients.
2. Stir in the beans and peas. Cover and cook on low for 5-7 hours or until onion and peppers are tender. Discard bay leaves.

Nutritional Value (Amount per Serving):

Calories: 152; Fat: 0.96; Carb: 30.23; Protein: 6.93

Crock Pot Vegan Quinoa and Mixed Bean Casserole

Prep Time: 20 Mins   Cook Time: 4 Hours   Serves: 4

Ingredients:

- 1 cup wild rice
- 3 cups vegetable broth
- 2 cups sliced mushrooms
- 1 onion, diced
- 2 cloves garlic, minced
- 1/4 cup chopped fresh parsley
- 2 tablespoons olive oil
- Salt and pepper to taste

Directions:

1. In the crock pot, combine wild rice, vegetable broth, sliced mushrooms,

diced onion, minced garlic, chopped fresh parsley, olive oil, salt, and pepper.

2. Stir well, cover, and cook on low for 4 hours or until the rice is tender.
3. Fluff with a fork before serving as a delightful pilaf.

Nutritional Value (Amount per Serving):

Calories: 231; Fat: 7.28; Carb: 36.68; Protein: 6.72

Slow Cooker Hobo Beans

Prep Time: 20 Mins   Cook Time: 6 Hours   Serves: 8

Ingredients:

- 1 large (28-ounce) can pork beans
- 1 (15-ounce) can red beans, or kidney beans, drained slightly
- 1 (15-ounce) can lima beans, or black-eyed peas, drained slightly
- 1 pound ground beef, cooked and drained
- 1 pound bacon, cubed, cooked, and drained
- 1 cup chopped onions
- 1 1/2 cups barbecue sauce

Directions:

1. Gather the ingredients.
2. Mix all—pork beans, red or kidney beans (whichever using), lima beans or black-eyed peas (whichever using), cooked and drained ground beef, cooked, drained and cubed bacon, onions, barbecue sauce—in a slow cooker.
3. Cook 5 to 6 hours on low.

Nutritional Value (Amount per Serving):

Calories: 477; Fat: 23.9; Carb: 41.53; Protein: 26.72

Slow Cooker Calico Beans

Prep Time: 15 Mins   Cook Time: 3 Hours 12 Mins   Serves: 10-12

Ingredients:

- 8 ounces bacon, about 10 to 12 slices
- 1 to 1 1/2 pounds lean ground beef (85 percent or better)
- 1 cup coarsely chopped onion
- 1/2 cup packed light brown sugar
- 1 tablespoon dry mustard
- 2 (15-ounce) cans baked beans
- 1 can lima beans, or butter beans, drained

- 1 can kidney beans, drained
- 1/2 cup ketchup, or barbecue sauce
- 1 tablespoon cider vinegar, or white vinegar
- Kosher salt, to taste
- Freshly ground black pepper, to taste

Directions:

1. Gather the ingredients.
2. Ina large skillet over medium-low heat, cook the bacon until just crisp. You can either cook the bacon whole or cut the bacon into chunks before cooking. Once crisp, remove the bacon to paper towels to drain. Leave about 2 teaspoons of bacon drippings in the skillet and discard the remaining drippings.
3. Place the skillet back over medium heat and add the ground beef and chopped onion. Cook until the beef is no longer pink, stirring and breaking up larger chunks. With a slotted spoon or spatula, transfer the ground beef to the crockery insert of the slow cooker.
4. Add the bacon, brown sugar, dry mustard, baked beans, lima beans, kidney beans, ketchup or barbecue sauce, and vinegar. Taste and season with kosher salt and freshly ground black pepper.
5. Cover and cook on low for 3 to 5 hours.

Nutritional Value (Amount per Serving):

Calories: 315; Fat: 19.78; Carb: 11.24; Protein: 23.08

Slow-Cooked Chili Beans

Prep Time: 15 Mins   Cook Time: 6 Hours   Serves: 6

Ingredients:

- 2 cups dried pinto beans, soaked overnight and drained
- 1 lb ground beef (or plant-based alternative)
- 1 onion, diced
- 2 cloves garlic, minced
- 1 can (14 oz) diced tomatoes
- 2 tablespoons chili powder
- 1 teaspoon cumin
- Salt and pepper to taste

Directions:

1. In a skillet, brown the ground beef over medium-high heat. Drain excess fat.
2. Place soaked beans, browned beef, diced onion, minced garlic, diced tomatoes, chili powder, cumin, salt, and pepper in the crock pot.
3. Stir well, cover, and cook on low for 6 hours.

4. Serve hot with your favorite toppings, such as shredded cheese, sour cream, or chopped green onions.

Nutritional Value (Amount per Serving):

Calories: 441; Fat: 13.59; Carb: 45.57; Protein: 33.96

Slow-Cooked Spinach and Chickpea Curry

Prep Time: 20 Mins   Cook Time: 4 Hours   Serves: 4

Ingredients:

- 2 cans (15 oz each) chickpeas, drained and rinsed
- 2 cups fresh spinach leaves
- 1 onion, diced
- 2 cloves garlic, minced
- 1 can (14 oz) diced tomatoes
- 1 can (14 oz) coconut milk
- 2 tablespoons curry powder
- Salt and pepper to taste
- Cooked rice for serving

Directions:

1. In the crock pot, combine chickpeas, fresh spinach leaves, diced onion, minced garlic, diced tomatoes, coconut milk, curry powder, salt, and pepper.
2. Stir well, cover, and cook on low for 4 hours.
3. Serve over cooked rice.

Nutritional Value (Amount per Serving):

Calories: 226; Fat: 4.78; Carb: 38.02; Protein: 10.92

Crock-Pot Vegetarian Moroccan Tagine

Prep Time: 15 Mins   Cook Time: 6 Hours   Serves: 6

Ingredients:

- 1 tablespoon extra virgin olive oil
- 1 medium yellow onion (peeled and diced)
- 3 cloves garlic (peeled and minced)
- 1 medium butternut squash (peeled, seeded and diced)
- 30 ounce canned Garbanzo Beans (drained and rinsed)
- 29 ounces canned fire roasted tomatoes (with juice)
- 2 medium carrots (peeled and diced)

- 18 ounces vegetable broth
- 1 tablespoon granulated sugar
- 1 tablespoon lemon juice
- 1 teaspoon ground coriander
- 1 teaspoon Kosher salt
- 1 teaspoon ground chili powder

Directions:

1. Heat a medium skillet over medium-high heat on the stove-top. Add the olive oil, and saute the onion and garlic in the oil until the onion is translucent.
2. Add the cooked onion, garlic and remaining ingredients to a 6 quart or larger slow cooker and stir to combine.
3. Cover and cook on LOW for 6 to 8 hours or until the carrots and butternut squash are tender.
4. Serve plain, or over cooked couscous or rice if desired.
5. Dig in and enjoy!

Nutritional Value (Amount per Serving):

Calories: 278; Fat: 6.56; Carb: 46.3; Protein: 11.8

Slow Cooker Beans and Ham

Prep Time: 20 Mins   Cook Time: 8 Hours   Serves: 8

Ingredients:

- 1 pound navy beans
- 1 Tablespoon minced garlic
- 1 diced onion
- 4 oz. baby carrots
- 1 pound ham and ham bone
- 1/2 teaspoon salt
- 1/2 teaspoon black pepper
- 1 Tablespoon parsley
- 32 oz. chicken broth
- 2 cups water

Directions:

1. Rinse the beans with water and look for rocks or any debris and remove it.
2. Add the beans, ham, garlic, onion, salt, pepper, and parsley to the slow cooker.
3. Pour the chicken broth and water over the ingredients and stir a little.
4. Place the lid on top and cook for 8 hours on low heat.
5. After eight hours, remove the bone, shred the ham, and serve.

Nutritional Value (Amount per Serving):

Calories: 456; Fat: 11.86; Carb: 39.79; Protein: 47.45

Chapter 9: Desserts

Crock Pot Apple Butter

Prep Time: 25 Mins   Cook Time: 5 Hours   Serves: 15

Ingredients:

- 5 lbs. apples
- 1 cup brown sugar packed
- 1 Tbsp. ground cinnamon
- 1/2 tsp. ground nutmeg
- 1/4 tsp. ground cloves
- 2 dashes salt

Directions:

1. Peel, core and slice the apples.
2. Add the apples to the slow cooker. Add the brown sugar, cinnamon, nutmeg, cloves, and salt.
3. Stir.
4. Cover and cook on HIGH for 5 hours or LOW for 8-10 hours.
5. After the apples have cooked, place them and any liquid that the apples made into a blender, cover with lid, and a towel on top of that (to prevent burns, in case the lid flies off). Hold the lid on while the blender is on. Pulse for about a minute, until very smooth.

Nutritional Value (Amount per Serving):

Calories: 139; Fat: 0.44; Carb: 35.72; Protein: 0.81

Crock Pot Peach Cobbler

Prep Time: 15 Mins   Cook Time: 3 Hours   Serves: 6

Ingredients:

- 4 cups sliced fresh or canned peaches
- 1 cup all-purpose flour
- 1 cup granulated sugar
- 1 tsp baking powder
- 1/4 tsp salt
- 1/2 cup milk
- 1/4 cup unsalted butter, melted
- 1 tsp vanilla extract
- Vanilla ice cream for serving (optional)

Directions:

1. Place the sliced peaches in the greased crock pot.
2. In a mixing bowl, whisk together flour, sugar, baking powder, and salt.
3. Stir in milk, melted butter, and vanilla extract until the batter is smooth.
4. Spoon the batter evenly over the peaches in the crock pot.
5. Cover and cook on low for 3 hours, or until the cobbler is bubbly and the top is golden brown.
6. Serve warm with a scoop of vanilla ice cream, if desired.

Crock Pot Chocolate Cherry Dump Cake

Prep Time: 10 Mins   Cook Time: 3 Hours   Serves: 10

Ingredients:

- 42 oz. cherry pie filling (two 21-oz. cans)
- 15.25 oz. chocolate cake mix
- 1 cup salted butter (2 sticks) melt in microwave

Directions:

1. Spray the slow cooker with non stick spray or rub with oil or crisco.
2. Add the cherry pie filling to the slow cooker, spread out to an even layer.
3. In a medium-size bowl combine the cake mix and melted butter. Only mix until just combined.
4. Add this cake mixture on top of the cherries in dollops, then spread out in an even layer.
5. Place the lid on the slow cooker.
6. Cook on high for 2 hours and 45 minutes to 3 hours or until the cake is set.
7. Serve warm with ice cream or whipped cream.

Nutritional Value (Amount per Serving):

Calories: 469; Fat: 22.01; Carb: 68.01; Protein: 2.62

Slow-Cooked Gingered Pears

Prep Time: 35 Mins   Cook Time: 4 Hours   Serves: 6

Ingredients:

- 1/2 cup finely chopped crystallized ginger
- 1/4 cup packed brown sugar
- 1/4 cup chopped pecans
- 1-1/2 teaspoons grated lemon zest
- 6 medium Bartlett or Anjou pears
- 2 tablespoons butter, cubed
- Optional: Vanilla ice cream and caramel ice cream topping

Directions:

1. In a small bowl, combine the ginger, brown sugar, pecans and zest.
2. Using a melon baller or long-handled spoon, core pears to within 1/4 in. of bottom. Spoon ginger mixture into the center of each pear.

3. Place pears upright in a slow cooker. Top each with butter. Cover and cook on low for 4-5 hours or until tender. If desired, serve with ice cream and caramel topping.

Nutritional Value (Amount per Serving):

Calories: 217; Fat: 7.27; Carb: 37.66; Protein: 1.28

Crock Pot Pumpkin Bread

Prep Time: 15 Mins   Cook Time: 3 Hours 30 Mins   Serves: 8

Ingredients:

- 1 3/4 cups all-purpose flour
- 1 tsp baking soda
- 1/2 tsp baking powder
- 1/2 tsp salt
- 1/2 tsp ground cinnamon
- 1/2 tsp ground nutmeg
- 1/4 tsp ground cloves
- 1/4 tsp ground allspice
- 1/2 cup unsalted butter, softened
- 1 cup granulated sugar
- 1/4 cup brown sugar
- 2 large eggs
- 1 (15 oz) can pumpkin puree
- 1/4 cup milk
- 1 tsp vanilla extract
- 1/2 cup chopped walnuts (optional)

Directions:

1. Grease the inside of the crock pot.
2. In a mixing bowl, whisk together flour, baking soda, baking powder, salt, cinnamon, nutmeg, cloves, and allspice.
3. In another bowl, cream together softened butter, granulated sugar, and brown sugar until light and fluffy.
4. Beat in eggs one at a time, then stir in pumpkin puree, milk, and vanilla extract.
5. Gradually add the dry mixture to the wet mixture and mix until just combined. Optionally, fold in chopped walnuts.
6. Pour the batter into the crock pot.
7. Cover and cook on low for 3 hours and 30 minutes or until a toothpick inserted into the center comes out clean.
8. Allow the pumpkin bread to cool before serving.

Nutritional Value (Amount per Serving):

Calories: 339; Fat: 14.5; Carb: 46.05; Protein: 7.17

Slow Cooker Berry Crumble

Prep Time: 15 Mins   Cook Time: 3 Hours   Serves: 8-10

Ingredients:

- 3/4 cup all purpose flour
- 3/4 cup quick cooking oats
- 1/4 cup + 2 tablespoons Truvia Brown Sugar Blend
- 1 teaspoon ground cinnamon
- 1/4 teaspoon salt
- 6 tablespoons unsalted butter
- 1/2 mini chocolate chips optional
- 3 cups frozen blueberries
- 2 cups frozen strawberries
- 1/4 cup Truvia Baking Blend
- 1 tablespoon lemon juice
- 2 tablespoons cornstarch

Directions:

1. Whisk flour, oats, Truvia Brown Sugar Blend, cinnamon, and salt in a large bowl. Dice butter into small chunks and add to the mixture, cutting it in with a pastry cutter until the mixture is crumbly. Stir in chocolate chips, if using. Set aside.
2. Rinse the frozen fruit to get rid of any ice chunks or crystals. Place in a second large bowl.
3. Sprinkle the Truvia Baking Blend, lemon juice, and cornstarch over the berries and toss to coat.
4. Spray the bottom of a 5-7 quart slow cooker with nonstick cooking spray. Add the fruit and juices, then top with the crumble topping.
5. Place a paper towel over the slow cooker opening, then cover with the lid. Cook on high power for approximately 2 1/2 to 3 hours, or until the top is wet looking (no powdery mixture remains) and the edges are bubbly.
6. Serve warm with low-sugar ice cream or whipped topping.

Nutritional Value (Amount per Serving):

Calories: 185; Fat: 7.46; Carb: 28.22; Protein: 2.66

Slow Cooker Bread and Butter Pudding

Prep Time: 10 Mins   Cook Time: 3 Hours   Serves: 6

Ingredients:

- 400 g white sliced bread 8-10 slices from a small (400 g/1 lb) loaf
- 65 g dried mixed fruit
- 2 tsp caster sugar
- 2 tsp caster sugar
- 1 tsp lemon zest
- 1/4 tsp ground cinnamon
- 300 ml double cream
- 150 ml milk
- 2 eggs

Directions:

1. Butter the bread, cut the slices into triangles and layer in the base of the slow cooker. Sprinkle over half the dried fruit and 1 tsp of caster sugar.
2. Layer up the rest of the bread, top with the rest of the dried fruit and 1 tsp

caster sugar.

3. Beat together the cream, milk and two eggs in a jug, pour it over the ingredients in the pot. Sprinkle with 2 tsp caster sugar, dust with cinnamon and 1 tsp lemon zest.

4. Press the ingredients down so that more of the bread is in the custard and will become deliciously soft during baking.

5. Put a tea towel under the lid and cook on high for 2-3 hours. A knife inserted can help you check if the custard is cooked through and firm.

6. Serve warm with custard, pouring cream or vanilla ice cream for a delicious cozy dessert.

Nutritional Value (Amount per Serving):

Calories: 343; Fat: 21.67; Carb: 30.5; Protein: 7.2

Slow Cooker Spiced Poached Pears

Prep Time: 25 Mins   Cook Time: 4 Hours   Serves: 8

Ingredients:

- 1-1/2 cups dry red wine or cranberry juice
- 1/3 cup packed brown sugar
- 2 tablespoons dried cherries
- 1 tablespoon ground cinnamon
- 1 whole star anise
- 1 dried Sichuan peppercorn, optional
- 4 ripe Boschpears
- 6 ounces bittersweet chocolate, chopped
- 1/4 cup heavy whipping cream
- 2 tablespoons pine nuts
- Fresh blackberries
- Sweetened whipped cream, optional

Directions:

1. In a slow cooker, mix wine, brown sugar, cherries, cinnamon, star anise and, if desired, peppercorn until blended. Peel and cut pears lengthwise in half. Remove cores, leaving a small well in the center of each. Arrange pears in wine mixture.

2. Cook, covered, on low 4-5 hours or until pears are almost tender. Discard star anise and peppercorn.

3. Place chocolate in a small bowl. In a small saucepan, bring cream just to a boil. Pour over chocolate; stir with a whisk until smooth.

4. To serve, remove pears to dessert dishes; drizzle with some of the poaching liquid. Spoon ganache into wells of pears. Top with pine nuts and blackberries. If desired, serve with whipped cream.

Nutritional Value (Amount per Serving):

Calories: 281; Fat: 2.25; Carb: 67.34; Protein: 1.48

Coconut Mango Bread Pudding with Rum Sauce

Prep Time: 30 Mins   Cook Time: 3 Hours   Serves: 6

Ingredients:

- 4 large eggs, beaten
- 1 can (13.66 ounces) coconut milk
- 1/3 cup packed brown sugar
- 1 teaspoon rum extract
- 1/2 teaspoon vanilla extract
- 1/2 teaspoon ground cinnamon
- 4 cups torn French bread
- 1/3 cup chopped dried mangoes
- 1/4 cup unsweetened coconut flakes, toasted
- 1/4 cup butter
- 1/2 cup packed brown sugar
- 2 tablespoons water
- 1 large egg yolk, beaten
- 1/2 teaspoon rum extract
- Toasted unsweetened coconut flakes, optional

Directions:

1. In a large bowl, whisk the first 6 ingredients until blended. Gently stir in bread, mangoes and coconut flakes. Transfer to a greased slow cooker. Cook, covered, on low until puffed and edges are dark golden, about 3 hours.
2. In a small heavy saucepan, heat butter and brown sugar over medium-low heat until blended. Whisk in water and yolk. Cook and stir until mixture is slightly thickened and a thermometer reads 175°F, about 10 minutes. Do not allow to boil. Immediately transfer to a bowl; stir in rum extract. Serve warm bread pudding with rum sauce. If desired, top with additional coconut.

Nutritional Value (Amount per Serving):

Calories: 431; Fat: 24.11; Carb: 50.12; Protein: 5.69

Crock Pot Butterscotch Pudding Cake

Prep Time: 15 Mins   Cook Time: 2 Hours 30 Mins   Serves: 8

Ingredients:

- 1 cup flour
- 3 oz cook-and-serve butterscotch pudding mix
- 1/4 cup sugar
- 2 tsp baking powder
- 1/2 tsp salt
- 3/4 cup milk
- 2 tbsp. vegetable oil
- 1 tbsp. vanilla extract

- 3/4 cup butterscotch chips
- 3 tbsp. butterscotch sauce
- 1/2 cup sugar
- 1 1/3 cup boiling water

Directions:

1. Spray the inside of a slow cooker bowl with nonstick cooking spray and set aside.
2. In a medium bowl, add flour, pudding mix, sugar, baking powder and salt. Whisk together until well combined. Make a well in the center.
3. To the center of the well in the dry ingredients, add milk, vegetable oil and vanilla. Stir until combined and batter is smooth.
4. Stir in butterscotch chips, and then pour batter into slow cooker.
5. In a small bowl, combine butterscotch sauce, sugar and boiling water. Stir until smooth, and then slowly and evenly pour over cake batter.
6. Cover and cook on high for 2.5 hours. When cooking time is done, leave lid on and let sit for 30 minutes.
7. To serve, remove a piece of the cake, and then add vanilla ice cream or whipped cream if desired. Spoon the sauce from the bottom of the slow cooker to drizzle over top.

Nutritional Value (Amount per Serving):

Calories: 267; Fat: 9.51; Carb: 41.07; Protein: 3.92

Crock Pot Apple Crisp

Prep Time: 15 Mins   Cook Time: 2 Hours 30 Mins   Serves: 10

Ingredients:

- 8 green apples cored, peeled and sliced
- 1/2 tsp cinnamon
- 1 1/4 c flour
- 3/4 c old fashioned oats
- 1 1/2 c brown sugar
- 1 tbsp cornstarch
- 1/4 tsp salt
- 1/4 c walnuts optional
- 1/3 c raisins optional
- 4 tbsp butter
- 3/4 c apple juice or cider

Directions:

1. Core, peel and thinly slice your apples (a bit thicker makes them a bit firmer, really thin makes it mushier). I peel half of the peels off because I like the taste, up to you if you want all peels off. Put them in a bowl.
2. Mix together your cinnamon, 3/4 c of flour, 1/2 c. oatmeal, 1 c. brown sugar and your cornstarch. (add raisins and/or walnuts if desired)
3. Add your apples and fold together until all apples slices are coated well.
4. Spray the inside of your crockpot with non stick spray, or use a liner.

5. Pour apple mixture inside. Pour apple juice/cider on top of them.
6. In another bowl, mix together 1/2 c. of flour, 1/2 c. brown sugar, salt, your butter – melted, and the remaining of your old fashioned oats 1/4 c.
7. Sprinkle this mixture on top of the apples in your slow cooker.
8. Put lid on and set to low for 2-1/2 hours.
9. Serve as is, or top with vanilla ice cream.

Nutritional Value (Amount per Serving):

Calories: 303; Fat: 7.26; Carb: 61.02; Protein: 3.51

Crock Pot Cocoa Almonds

Prep Time: 15 Mins   Cook Time: 1 Hour 30 Mins   Serves: 2

Ingredients:

- 2 cups almonds
- 2 tablespoons butter, cut into pieces
- 1/8 teaspoon powdered stevia extract (or 1/3 cup sugar)
- 1 teaspoon vanilla
- 1-2 tablespoons cocoa powder
- Dash salt or use salted almonds

Directions:

1. Combine nuts, stevia, vanilla, cocoa, and salt in a crock pot.
2. Lay pats of butter on top.
3. Cover and cook on HIGH for one hour.
4. Stir and cook another 30 minutes.
5. Stir and pour out on wax paper to cool.

Nutritional Value (Amount per Serving):

Calories: 139; Fat: 12.7; Carb: 6.74; Protein: 1.44

Burgundy Pears

Prep Time: 10 Mins   Cook Time: 3 Hours   Serves: 6

Ingredients:

- 6 medium ripe pears
- 1/3 cup sugar
- 1/3 cup Burgundy wine or grape juice
- 3 tablespoons orange marmalade
- 1 tablespoon lemon juice
- 1/4 teaspoon ground cinnamon

- 1/4 teaspoon ground nutmeg
- Dash salt
- Vanilla ice cream

Directions:

1. Peel pears, leaving stems intact. Core from the bottom. Stand pears upright in a slow cooker. In a small bowl, combine the sugar, wine or grape juice, marmalade, lemon juice, cinnamon, nutmeg and salt. Carefully pour over pears.
2. Cover and cook on low for 3-4 hours or until tender. To serve, drizzle pears with sauce and garnish with vanilla ice cream.

Nutritional Value (Amount per Serving):

Calories: 274; Fat: 0.76; Carb: 70.11; Protein: 1.13

Crock Pot Banana Foster

Prep Time: 15 Mins   Cook Time: 2 Hours   Serves: 12

Ingredients:

- 12 bananas, cut into quarters
- 1 cup flaked coconut
- 1 cup dark corn syrup
- 2/3 cup butter, melted
- ¼ cup lemon juice
- 2 teaspoons grated lemon peel
- 2 teaspoons rum
- 1 teaspoon ground cinnamon
- ½ teaspoon salt
- 12 slices prepared pound cake
- 1 quart vanilla ice cream

Directions:

1. Combine bananas and coconut in Crock pot. Combine corn syrup, butter, lemon juice, lemon peel, rum, cinnamon and salt in medium bowl; stir to blend. Pour over bananas.
2. Coverand cook on LOW 1 to 2 hours. To serve, arrange bananas on pound cake slices. Top with ice cream and warm sauce.

Nutritional Value (Amount per Serving):

Calories: 614; Fat: 12.66; Carb: 130.42; Protein: 5.95

APPENDIX RECIPE INDEX

Made in the USA
Las Vegas, NV
12 May 2024

89856994R00063